POODLES

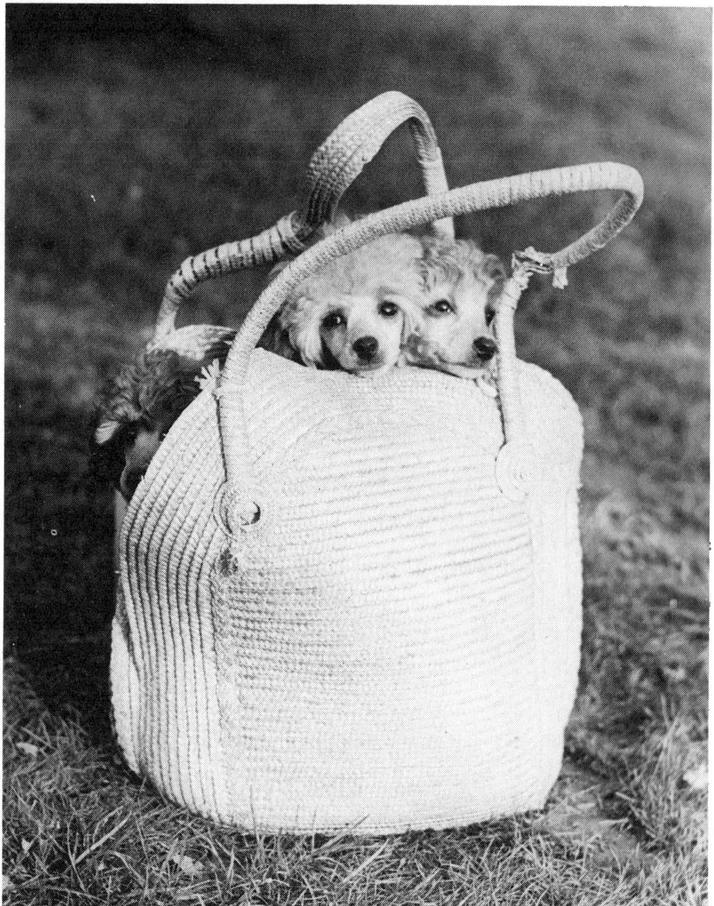

POODLES

BY

MARGARET ROTHERY SHELDON
AND
BARBARA LOCKWOOD

ARCO PUBLISHING COMPANY, INC.
NEW YORK

© W. & G. Foyle Ltd. 1958
Published in the United States of America 1976 by
Arco Publishing Company, Inc.
219 Park Avenue South, New York, N.Y. 10003

Library of Congress Cataloging in Publication Data
Sheldon, Margaret Rothery.
　Poodles.

　(Arco/Foyles pet handbooks)
　Bibliography:　p.
　Includes index.
　1.　Poodles.　I.　Lockwood, Barbara, joint author.
II.　Title.
SF429.P85S53　　1976　　　　636.7'2　　　　76–11005
ISBN 0–668–03974–4

Printed in Great Britain

This book is dedicated to CHAMPION ROTHARA THE GAMINE, daughter of USA/CH. ROTHARA THE CAVALIER, and dam of USA/CH. ROTHARA THE RAGAMUFFIN.

ACKNOWLEDGMENTS

The Authors wish to extend their grateful thanks to Mrs. Margaret Worth of the Piccoli Poodles for some of the photographs; to Miss Margaret Sherson for typing the manuscript; and to all others who have been so helpful and lent photographs.

CONTENTS

Chapter		Page
	FOREWORD	9
1	EARLY POODLE HISTORY	11
2	POODLE FASHIONS	14
3	CHOOSING A POODLE PUPPY	18
4	REARING THE YOUNG POODLE	23
5	TRAINING THE POODLE	29
6	CARE OF THE POODLE COAT	35
7	POODLE CLIPPING	38
8	POODLE BREEDING	44
9	THE FIRST POODLE LITTER	51
10	THE SMALL KENNEL OF POODLES	61
11	DOG SHOWS AND PROCEDURE	65
12	SOME POODLE TALES	73
13	POODLES AND OBEDIENCE TRAINING	81
Appendix I	THE KENNEL CLUB STANDARD OF THE BREED	87
Appendix II	POODLE CLUBS OF GREAT BRITAIN	89
Appendix III	BIBLIOGRAPHY	92
	INDEX	93

FOREWORD

It is a great pleasure for me to write a short Foreword for this book on Poodles written by Mrs. Sheldon and Miss Lockwood.

I notice that the book is primarily intended as a handbook for the novice Poodle owner. There have been many books written about Poodles but little has been done for the novices to the breed, who must number many tens of thousands.

I have known the Authors for a long time and I am sure that they feel, as I do, that the Poodle should always be a member of the family and have a place of honour in the home.

I wish the book every success.

MARGARET CAMPBELL INGLIS.

(Chairman of the International Poodle Club.)

1

EARLY POODLE HISTORY

*The First Poodles—The Rise in Popularity of the Miniatures—
Pioneering the Toy Poodle.*

THERE seems to be a certain amount of doubt as to the country of origin of the Poodle. The French would have us believe that the Poodle or "caniche" originated in France, but equally it is known that the "Pudel" was to be seen in Germany and Russia as early as 1553. But one of the first references to a Poodle in England appears to be in 1635, when Prince Rupert came to aid Charles I in fighting the Roundheads and brought with him his white Poodle "Boye".... The legend goes that "Boye" could speak many languages and that Prince Rupert frequently used to set him on his enemies, and this gallant dog finally was killed in the Battle of Marston Moor in 1643. There is an interesting reproduction of a picture showing this Poodle (which has the resemblance more of a lion) dated 1642, in Stanley Dangerfield's book *Your Poodle and Mine*. Another interesting lithograph also reproduced in this book is entitled *Les Tondenses de Chiens* by J. J. Chalon and dated 1820, showing two Frenchwomen busily clipping Poodles in the street, with several Poodles of varying colours, both chained up and in barred kennels awaiting their turn for trimming. This must surely have been the origin of what is now the smart town Beauty Parlour or Clipping Salon for Poodles. Another fascinating reproduction dated 1818, entitled "The Toy Poodle at Dinner", shows a very small white Poodle sitting up to the dining table and being handed a tasty morsel by his doting owner; and yet another is an amusing etching by Theodore Lane, dated 1820, called "Innocent Amusements", and here we see the maiden lady complete with mob cap and a love bird perched on the screen, carefully combing her white Poodle and rolling his hair in curl papers. Another more detailed study is one of back-stage life at the Circus or Fair in the painting by Ludwig Knaus, dated 1880, and entitled "Behind the Scenes". This shows three performing white Poodles obviously resting as near as they can to the old stove on which the family meal is cooking. These three reproductions all appear in *The Book of the Poodle* by T. H. Tracy.

The first Poodles were registered at the Kennel Club as early as 1875 and more were progressively registered each year until 1904 when Poodles were divided into two varieties; the Corded Poodles over 15in. and the non-Corded Poodles over 15in. The Corded Poodle was a curious looking dog with long hair which hung in tight cords. These cords were never combed out but were constantly dressed with oil which helped their growth to a fantastic length. The daily life of the Corded Poodle could hardly have been carefree, for the long cords rested 6in. or 7in. on the floor, and when the Poodle was not being shown, these cords were tied up in material bags. The cords fell from the middle of the back, with only slightly shorter cords hanging from the tail and the muzzle. The famous dog, Champion "Achilles", a big dog of 23in. with cords of 30in., owned by Mr. Chance, had the distinction of being made the first Poodle champion in 1890. Certain pioneering breeders were endeavouring to reduce the size of Poodles and produce a miniature, and in 1911 the first Miniature Poodles were registered at the Kennel Club. Now—nearly fifty years later—enthusiastic breeders are again trying to reduce the size still further to produce a Toy Poodle under 11in., and already these little ones have received the recognition of the Kennel Club as a separate variety and have rightly come into their own.

Since the Second World War, Miniature Poodles have soared to great popularity in both England and America, and in 1949 we see that 2,641 were registered: the breed was placed twelfth on the list of all breeds registered at the Kennel Club for that year. In 1950 they move up three places with a registration total of 3,227 and are ninth on the list; in 1951 they step up yet another two places to the seventh with a registration of 3,984, overtaking both the smooth Dachshund and the Scottish Terrier in that year. In 1952 they rose to fourth on the register with 4,570 registrations, superseding Pembroke Corgis, Boxers and Wire Fox Terriers. One more step to third place in 1953, with a total of 6,322 registrations, usurps the position held for the last four years by the ever-

EARLY POODLE HISTORY

popular Pekinese. In 1954 and 1955 Miniature Poodles reached the summit with registration totals of 8,632 and 12,198 respectively, sending Cocker Spaniels and Alsatians down to second and third places. In 1956, the number of Miniature Poodles registered was 16,995—more than double second and third places respectively. In 1957 and 1958 the Poodle Miniature registrations were 18,340 and 21,239, with Toy Poodles appearing with registrations of 2,169 and 4,590. In 1959, for the sixth year running, Miniatures topped the breed register and this time with a registration of 22,541, with Toy Poodles coming along in fifth place with 7,132 registrations. But is this a happy state of affairs for the Miniature Poodle? For while there are a great many honest and reputable breeders who have the well-being of the Poodle deep in their hearts, there are also those who have commercialized the breed and almost mass-produced a large number of inferior specimens purely for their cash value. If readers are planning to commence breeding this completely delightful breed of dog, they should be certain they obtain their foundation stock from a reputable breeder who is to be trusted. To find a reliable breeder in the first place, advice may be sought from the Secretary of the Kennel Club, Clarges Street, Piccadilly, London, W.1, or any of the Secretaries of the various Poodle Clubs listed farther on in this book. The outstanding characteristics of this lovely breed of dog are, above all, its intelligence, its elegance, its sensitivity, and its companionship, and it would be a tragedy if these fine qualities were lost forever through careless and ill-advised breeding.

2

POODLE FASHIONS

Sizes of Poodles—Various Clipping Styles—Colours of Modern Poodles.

There are three sizes of Poodles known in England, and recognized by the English Kennel Club. First, there is the large variety, sometimes erroneously referred to as the "Standard" Poodle. The size of this poodle must be not less than 15in. at the shoulder, and the correct term for this variety is the "Poodle". Before the First World War this variety was moderately popular, both in the show ring and as companions. But about the beginning of the century a few breeders wished to evolve a smaller Poodle, and by careful and selective breeding they began to produce the first of the Miniature Poodles which are so popular to-day. The endeavour of the breeders of Miniature Poodles was, of course, to produce a miniature Poodle of about half the size of the Poodle; in fact one that was under 15in. at the shoulder, but which retained all the elegance and style of the larger Poodle. At first these new Miniatures lost much in type and did not bear much resemblance to the fine elegance and real beauty of some of the top Miniatures of the present day. But a great deal of pioneer work was done and slowly a lovely Miniature Poodle was evolved which had all the attributes of the larger Poodle and was losing the bad points which had appeared when the size was first being reduced. At the present time, very much the same procedure is being followed in the attempt to breed a yet smaller variety of Poodle—a variety which must be under 11in. at the shoulder—as was originally carried out when Miniatures were in their infancy. This variety is now referred to as the "Toy" Poodle, and received official status from the Kennel Club early in 1957. In America, Toys have been recognized as a separate variety for some years but the size limit is even less—only 10in. at the shoulder. Again, Toy Poodles have a long way to go before they attain the elegance and beauty of both the Poodle and the Miniature, but a lot of concentrated study and careful breeding is being carried out and there is no reason why this tiny "miniature" Miniature should not equal its larger brothers and sisters in quality in the not too distant future.

There are many stories of how the various clips came into being, and perhaps the most likely to be authentic regarding the traditional Lion Clip is that in the early days the Poodle was extensively used as a duck-shooting dog, and was required to work in the reeds. To facilitate movement in the water, the lower half of his body and his legs were shaved of hair, but as a means of protection against rheumatism and cold, the large mane was left which covered most of the vital internal organs. For the same reason the hair was left round the wrist joints of the fore legs, and ankle joints of the back legs. To enable sportsmen to see their dogs working, a red ribbon was tied on the top-knot and the end of the pom on the tail, for in those days the tail was long and undocked. Legend has it that then the French clowns adopted Poodles in the circuses and travelling shows because of their intelligence and great aptitude for learning tricks and when this came about, the "poms" on the head, legs and tail (which was now docked) were exaggerated to resemble the poms on the clowns' traditional clothing. This Lion Clip has come down through the ages, and is often referred to as the Traditional Clip, and is the accepted clip for dogs of a year and older which are exhibited in the show ring to-day, and while not enforcing it, the Kennel Club recommends that this clip shall be used. However, the more recent Dutch or Modern Clip may be used in the ring as there is no actual rule against it and indeed in many shows there are classes especially scheduled for this type of clip. If a Poodle in Dutch or Modern Clip competes against a Poodle in the traditional Lion Clip he starts at a disadvantage however, as he may lose the fifteen points theoretically awarded for *length* of coat, as in a smart Modern Clip the hair is kept to a length of not more than 1in. to 1½in. on any part of the dog, except perhaps on the head and the tail "pom". Modern Clip seems to have been designed as the distinct opposite in every detail to the Lion Clip, for in the former the hair is left longer on both fore and back legs, while the body and neck are cropped as close as possible.

There is no doubt that Modern or Dutch Clip is smart, chic and ultra-fashionable, but one cannot help feeling that it does not show off the fine bone, elegant gait and sheer line of beauty of the Poodle to the extent apparent in the Lion Clip. But this is a highly controversial subject and there is obviously a great deal both for and against both kinds of Clip. For good working country clothes the Poodle is probably better off in the sober Lamb or Curly Trim, which is a short all-over cut, of about ½in. to 1in. long, with just the feet, face and tail shaved close.

Very stringent rules regarding the colour of Poodles are laid down by the Kennel Club, and the relevant paragraph of the Kennel Club Standard states "*Colour*: All black, all white, all brown, all blue and all solid colours." The words "all solid colours" have quite recently been added and agreed upon, and cover such colours as silver, apricot and cream. But Poodles of any size which are in the slightest degree mis-marked or parti-coloured are much to be deplored, and it cannot be too highly stressed that when breeding Poodles, like colour should be mated with like colour. The only reason for deviating from this procedure is when an experienced breeder is experimenting with colours to produce a deeper, lighter, or better colour in any one particular strain, in which case such a breeder will take careful steps to ensure that any mis-marked or parti-coloured progeny will not be bred from and probably will be sold without a pedigree with this proviso. For instance, if a black is mated with a white the resulting puppies can only be hybrids in colour, and although they may all be black themselves they now carry parti-coloured genes, and may themselves throw mismarks. This is a vast subject and there is not space in this booklet to investigate all aspects of colour-breeding, but the novice breeder will be well advised at any rate to play safe by mating like colour with like colour, for a mating of black to brown may produce a percentage of rusty blacks, while black to silver or blue may produce bad, slaty blacks; white and apricot may produce whites with deep apricot ears.

Quite a number of white puppies may be born with *slightly* tinged ears, but these clear in colour as the puppies mature provided that the sire and dam were pure white or cream and descended from pure white or cream lines. But if an apricot colour has been introduced to the white line, the chances are that the ears of the puppies will not clear in colour. A rusty or slaty black on the other hand will appear jet black until possibly ten or twelve months old, before beginning to turn a bad colour. Brown Poodles mated with Silver Poodles often produce puppies which when mature turn into *cafe-au-lait* colour which can hardly be called a solid colour. Silver Poodles are usually born black, but begin to turn silver on the face and paws at quite an early age, and if the roots of the hair are closely examined, a sheen of silver will be noticed to be growing up. Apricots, if they are to remain a good colour, should be almost black or a bronze with a sheen of gold, at birth. Whites are either born paper-white which means that they have a shell pink skin and in this case the black pigmentation takes longer to establish itself, or else they are born slightly off-white which means that they have a darker skin, very slightly tinged ears, and a quickly established black nose, pads and lips. Possibly the ideal is the paper-white at birth with jet black nose, eye rims, pads and lips, as puppies born with this combination retain this ideal pigmentation throughout their lives whatever the circumstances or conditions of weather, and can also generally be relied upon to pass on this attribute to their progeny. Black noses in white Poodles have always been a slightly difficult point, and the colour quite often goes "off" in the winter, possibly through lack of sunshine, or if the dog is slightly out of condition or lacking in vitamins. But here the safe rule is to use the white stud dog whose nose is really black and *whose progeny* have black noses, and it is more than likely then that no pigmentation trouble will be experienced.

3

CHOOSING A POODLE PUPPY

The points to look for in a pet puppy and the points of a Show Poodle—Importance of sound foundation stock.

UNLESS you are unable to do so for very good reasons, do go yourself to the kennels you have selected and see your puppy in his or her home surroundings; we consider this very important and certainly worth a little trouble. Most reputable breeders do not like selling their puppies to people they have not seen—perhaps this astonishes you, but now that Poodles are so fashionable not everyone who wishes to buy a puppy is, in the eyes of a breeder, suitable to have one. Everyone loves a puppy but, thinks the breeder, are these people going to care for it properly once its endearing puppy charms have waned? and if the answer is "No", then no amount of money will tempt that breeder to part with the puppy.

If on the other hand you are really unable to visit the kennels, you may safely leave the choice to any breeder recommended by the Kennel Club, or the various Poodle Clubs; write, stating clearly what your requirements are: age, sex, colour, whether for a companion or for a show specimen and the price you wish to pay. Remember you cannot buy a show quality puppy cheaply by stating you only want it for a pet, intending to show it later, and then blame the breeder when it does not win.

The price of good healthy well-reared pedigree Poodle puppies of about eight to twelve weeks old, from well kept stock, varies from fifteen guineas for pets, up to thirty five guineas for the top show quality, with perhaps a further rise in price for the exceptionally outstanding specimen.

The rearing of strong puppies these days is an expensive business with milk, eggs and meat at their present high prices, and remember, it will cost you just as much to rear a badly bred puppy as a good one, and you may be landed with vet's. bills as well, so it is well worth spending a little more on the initial outlay.

However, in order not to be taken in by unscrupulous people who are taking advantage of the present popularity of the Poodle by selling poor quality puppies at very high prices, it is as well that you should have a little knowledge of what to look for in your pup. An eight-week old puppy should be fat and gay, he should have a clear bright eye, he should be clean in coat and skin and feet; his skin should be loose and his stomach should not be distended, as this is a sign of worms. He should be energetic and friendly, though remember to give him time to get used to you. You can ask to see the parents, the breeder will be delighted to show them to you if they are members of the kennels. If you are purchasing a puppy for show ring purposes, ask the breeder to demonstrate the puppy's action for you. Be careful of colour. If you are considering starting a small kennel you must be extremely careful in the purchase of your foundation stock; any well-known breeder will be delighted to help you with advice, and in this case you will be wise to choose one of the really noted show winning kennels from which to purchase your first stock. You may have to pay a few pounds more for your puppy, and even wait a short while for the type you want, but remember you are also obtaining a pedigree bearing the names of reliable and well-known dogs, which will be a big selling point when you come to breed.

Before embarking on such a purchase it is well to gain as much knowledge as possible; study the standard of the breed, attend shows, talk to breeders, read books, and if possible take a short course in Poodle management in a Poodle kennel. One can waste so much time and money through lack of knowledge.

Of course in a young puppy it is not possible to be sure about all the following points, but even so we should be able to check on a great many of them.

The Poodle should be bright and intelligent, with marked elegance. A tendency to clumsy awkwardness with heavy bone should be avoided. If an older dog, he should have a distinctly proud and dignified look, and we must not expect him to rush at us immediately. He must take his time to get to know us and will probably regard us with a certain amount of tolerant aloofness until he is sure about us. His head should be lean and long with a really flat cheek. Roundness of cheek, lippiness (as in a spaniel) is incorrect. His eye should be dark and oval shaped, never round or protruding. A lighter eye in brown Poodles is acceptable. His ears should fall close to his head, and the leathers (flesh part) should be wide and long.

His teeth should be strong and white and correct in number. There should be in both upper and lower jaws, six incisors (small front teeth) which are sub-divided into "nippers" which are the two middle teeth, "intermediates" which are those next to the nippers, and "corners", these which come next. Then there is one large "canine" on either side of the six teeth. Behind these come the pre-molars and molars of which there are usually six on each side of the upper jaw, and seven on each side of the lower jaw, making in all forty-two teeth. When purchasing a dog of an age to have his permanent teeth, the number and correct placement should always be checked. The incisors and canines can also be checked in a young puppy though molars and pre-molars may not be through, but correct placement of teeth should have special attention.

Next, we come to the shoulders, and here the shoulder blade should slope backwards at quite an angle, and we should be able to draw an imaginary straight line down the ear and down the front leg to the ground if the Poodle has a well carried head. The head which pokes forward takes away all dignity and elegance from the Poodle. Chest should be deep and moderately wide, with a good barrel (well rounded ribs), while the back should be strong and slightly hollowed, never "roach" backed. The well-balanced Poodle should measure exactly the same from the nape of the neck to the root of the tail as he does from the top of the shoulder to the ground.

The loins must be broad and muscular though not actually heavy. For the hindquarters we must look for angulation, and by this is meant that the hind leg is well bent to allow of a really powerful thrust to the hind action. The back legs must never form a straight line from tail to ground, and the hock (or ankle) should be well let down and low to ground, and should extend out at the back. The tail should be moderately high set, that is right on the end of the backbone, and should be carried at an angle of about a 120°. If the tail is low set, the Poodle will have difficulty in getting it up to a cheerful angle. On the other hand, a Poodle must never have too gay a tail, or anything resembling that of a squirrel. The coat should be of strong hard texture and very thick and profuse, and of even length. He will acquire his adult coat possibly at eighteen months, though may not be in his prime until two-and-a-half to three years old. Up to eighteen months the coat may still be slightly soft and even a little silky. But at any age, the coat should be dense and never "open" or wispy.

Black toe-nails are much to be desired in a white Poodle, though they are rather the exception than the rule, and skins may be either silver or pink, but pink or liver coloured noses are a fault. Brown Poodles may have brown noses, but silver, black, blue and apricot Poodles should all have black noses and black toe-nails.

In France, white Poodles must have silver and not pink skins; and only the basic shades of black, white and brown Poodles are allowed in the show ring. Also no Poodles with back dew claws (or traces of these) may be exhibited on the Continent.

When purchasing a Poodle dog, we should examine him to be sure that he has two testicles, and is thus neither a monorchid (one testicle only) or a cryptorchid (neither testicle), for according to the Kennel Club this state of affairs precludes a dog from winning in England as it does in the United States.

A dog that is a monorchid is able to sire a litter, but a cryptorchid is completely sterile and cannot be used at stud.

It is now laid down that if a puppy or adult dog of any breed is to be exported from this country, a Kennel Club form must be signed certifying that the dog is neither a monorchid nor a cryptorchid. There is much controversy about this state of affairs and it is not established whether it is a matter of heredity, although many hold it is only carried through the female line. However, it should be checked when purchasing, and can be ascertained in a puppy as young as eight weeks.

Regarding the size of the Poodle, a Standard Poodle must be over 15in. at the shoulder and the usual size is at least 20in.; while a Miniature Poodle must be under 15in. at the shoulder. Toy Poodles, now officially recognized as a separate variety, must be under 11in. In the United States the sizes for the Standard and the Miniature are the same, but Toys must be under 10 in.

It is always wisest for the prospective breeder-exhibitor to start with a bitch rather than a dog, as when breeding time comes along this bitch can be put to a well known dog of her own blood lines and the resultant puppies, because of the breeding behind them, can command a good price even though the breeder is not yet well known. If the price of such a bitch puppy is beyond your means it is usually possible to arrange part breeding terms, by which you pay a lower price and undertake to bring her back to the breeder for mating, and give up one puppy or more of the resultant litter unregistered and free of charge. This is an excellent way to acquire a top quality specimen, which the breeder is not willing to sell outright.

In the case of the prospective kennel owner we would strongly recommend that you treat the financial side of your Poodles in a business-like way. It is our proud boast that except for the price of our first bitch puppy and her first stud fee no money has been put into our kennels and nothing has been bought that has not been paid for by the Poodles. This can easily be achieved if only the best possible stock is bought for foundation, and if ruthless care is taken over the selection of home bred stock to be retained. The dear little puppy with the glamorous eyes and sweet expression which takes your eye off its bad action, mouth or coat, will never be a money maker, and is better off in a nice home as a pet, rather than as an expensive passenger in your kennels.

If you do not feel competent to choose a top quality puppy or adult Poodle yourself, you can always take a knowledgeable friend with you if you wish, but breeders with a fine show-winning reputation are unlikely, if they are wise, to offer you anything but the best, since the dog will bear their prefix in its future show career.

4

REARING THE YOUNG POODLE

Temperature—Pulse—Worming—Distemper Immunisation—Care of Eyes, Ears and Feet.

You have chosen your Poodle and started to house train him and now you must turn your thoughts to steering your poodle puppy through his or her adolescence.

We have found that Poodles as a breed are extremely healthy and hardy, and suffer very few illnesses if fed and housed properly. But it is as well to know what to do in the first place if your puppy or adult should be off colour. You must know how to take his temperature, how to take his pulse, and how to give him a dose, either liquid or in tablet form. You must study him in health as well as in sickness so that any difference in normal behaviour will immediately be apparent to you and warn you that all is not well. For instance if your Poodle seems abnormally sleepy and does not want to come out of his bed; if he is more than usually thirsty and yet does not fancy his food; if his gums and tongue are pale in colour; if he vomits or has diarrhoea, however slight, these are signs that should warn the careful owner that something may be wrong. The first action should be to take his temperature, and so be sure that you have a blunt-nosed clinical thermometer handy. A dog's normal temperature is 101.2° F., but a puppy can be a degree higher quite happily and be quite fit. But anything above 103° F. very often spells trouble and you will need professional advice from your vet.

To take the temperature, grease the blunt silvered end of the thermometer with vaseline and insert very gently into the dog's rectum for about 1in. to 1½in. You must never use any force, and as long as the end of the thermometer is inside the rectum, the temperature will be correctly recorded. You should keep the thermometer inserted for at least a minute, then take it out, wipe with a piece of cotton wool and take the reading. At the same time you may wish to take the pulse, which is achieved by putting two fingers close up into the dog's groin. After a little practice you will soon feel the beat, and the normal pulse is between seventy and a hundred per minute. Get to know your Poodle's pulse in health as well as in sickness, bearing in mind that a dog's pulse beats irregularly and not entirely rhythmically, and you should know the "feel" and rhythm of his pulse long before he is actually ill.

To give him a dose of liquid medicine, take your Poodle gently between your knees and with the fingers of your left hand pull out the corner of his right under lip, and then slowly pour the spoonful of medicine into the small pocket of his mouth. To give pills, again hold him between your knees, open his mouth putting the pill right on the back of his tongue, close his mouth quickly and hold it closed, stroking his throat until you see him swallow. Again it pays to give your dog pills or tablets such as "Vetzyme" or other conditioners when he is quite well so that they hold no horrors for him.

Possibly the first problem will be that he needs worming. Undoubtedly his breeder will have wormed him at six weeks, but he will probably need another dose at about three months. Gone are the days of dreadful oily purges with hours of miserable starvation beforehand; worming in these enlightened days holds little horror. An excellent preparation is "Banocide" manufactured by Burroughs Wellcome. The dose is half a tablet to each 4lbs. of body weight and is given about ten minutes after a normal meal. Only one dose is usually necessary, and the tablets can only be obtained through your Veterinary Surgeon.

Your Poodle will by now have endeared himself to you considerably and no doubt you will be wondering how likely he is to pick up Hard Pad, Distemper or Hepatitis, or other infectious and contagious diseases. In the olden days we personally were not much in favour of the various immunising vaccines and protective serums, but since Burroughs Wellcome have produced "Epivax Plus", we really cannot recommend this too highly. There seems to be little doubt that this vaccine does give very lasting protection to dogs. You must, of course, call in your Veterinary Surgeon to give this innoculation, and the puppy should be immunised when over nine weeks old. Unlike the old vaccines, the puppy is not infectious after innoculation, but it should be borne in mind that he is rather more liable to pick up infection for a week or ten days after the

REARING THE YOUNG POODLE

injection until the immunisation has really built up. One injection gives life-long protection, and there appear to be no after effects. Before innoculation, and indeed at all times throughout his life, your Poodle should be guarded as far as is possible from all contact with any known or unknown infection. Keep him away from trees and lamp-posts and street corners where other dogs have been, do not take him into Pet shops; do not take him, unless compelled, to the vet's. surgery—ask your vet. to visit your house and invite him to wash his hands before he touches your Poodle. If you take him to a Show disinfect his feet and give him a small dose of T.C.P. diluted one part in eight parts water, before going into the Show and on leaving.

Distemper and Hard-pad are terrible diseases and every possible means should be taken to protect your Poodle from contractting either disease. However, if he suddenly appears sleepy, goes off his food, has a hot dry nose or an abnormally wet one, perhaps a little cough and slight congestion of the eyes, take his temperature at once. If it is high, it appears ominous and the quicker you can get veterinary advice the better. If he has no temperature it may be nothing, but watch him continually. In Distemper there is usually a very high temperature at the outset, and then this drops to normal and one relapses into false security; but in about ten days' time his temperature will rise again, and he will become really ill. If you have managed to keep him quiet and have regarded him as suspect throughout this ten days, feeding him on a light diet, he may never develop the second phase, and he may have only a very slight attack with no after effects. The symptoms of Distemper and Hard-pad are so very similar that it is often almost impossible to know the difference. It is said that in Hard-pad the nose is abnormally wet with a clear discharge, but in Distemper the discharge is thick and mucous. The golden rule in either disease is to starve your patient. If you can be strong-minded enough to give him nothing but plain boiled water and honey until his temperature comes down to normal, his stomach and internal organs will be pure and clean, and he will have used none of his precious energy in trying to digest food. Also the germs will have had nothing to feed upon. The more a dog has to eat at this time, the more chance the germs will have to multiply. However, in the case of any illness, keep your puppy warm and quiet, and give him nothing but honey and water pending the arrival of the Vet. with his expert knowledge and specific treatment.

During hot weather, or indeed in almost any weather, a dog can pick up fleas, lice and ticks quite easily from fields, other dogs, etc. To obviate any infestation such as the above, the house Poodle should be bathed quite frequently, and if there is any evidence of these pests, the coat can be dusted with "Gammexane" powder which is excellent. If your Poodles live in kennels be careful to use only wheat straw for bedding, as oat straw undoubtedly encourages lice, while the seeds from barley straw can cause much irritation and damage. Dust the sleeping boxes with "Izal" powder or "Gammexane" powder and change the straw every week.

At four months your Poodle will be cutting his adult teeth, and this may or may not be a trying time. One hears less and less these days of teething fits, or perhaps it is that Poodles are particularly free of them, but we have never experienced them in our own kennels. Should your puppy have a teething fit, splash cold water on his head and face, and keep him in a dark and cool place for a little while. During teething, he may go off his food quite considerably, and if you look at his gums you will probably find them very sore and inflamed. For a while until all teeth are through, give him softer food and that which is cut smaller than usual. He may also become very snappy and restless when being groomed or trimmed, which again is simply because his gums and face are so sore. When his teeth are finally through, they should be cleaned every week with damp cotton wool and a good tooth powder such as "Eucryl", or else swabbed round with cotton wool dipped in equal parts of Peroxide of Hydrogen and fresh milk. This latter is excellent for cleaning the teeth of show dogs.

Occasionally after clipping a Poodle puppy, or for that matter an adult Poodle, he may develop a "Clipper Rash". This is an unpleasant rash which irritates considerably, causing the Poodle to scratch until he makes a raw place. If your Poodle is prone to "Clipper Rash" dust the shaven parts with 20% Zinc Oxide in *sterilized* talcum powder immediately after clipping. Another good preventative is to anoint the shaven parts with "Johnson's Baby Lotion". But if your Poodle has been bathed *before* clipping, there is less likelihood of any rash.

Eyes should be kept clean, and a cotton wool swab in ordinary warm water is all that is usually necessary. If the eyes become inflamed from cold winds or any other slight cause, and are rather inclined to "weep", then a washing out with a solution of one teaspoonful of salt in one pint of warm water is very soothing. Sometimes eyes weep for no apparent reason, and this may be due to acidity. A course of any alkaline such as "Maclean's Milk of Magnesia" will work wonders. Your Poodle should be protected as much as possible from exposure to very cold winds, as this may set up painful earache. Care should also be taken that water does not get into the ear channel either when bathing or if they are out in the rain. Always take care to well dry the inside of the ear with cotton wool and dust with a good quality ear powder such as Bob Martin's, Sherley's or Spratts, all of which can be obtained in a puffer tin. For more longstanding and serious ear canker, the preparation "Ry-o-tin" made by the Rybar Laboratories is excellent, but the directions must be followed minutely for a resulting cure. But for all the troubles of ears and eyes it is better to consult your vet., as much harm can be done by the unskilled, though well meaning novice owner.

Poodles' feet need a certain amount of attention, and you should ensure that all hair between the toes is carefully clipped or cut out, otherwise the feet will lose their elegance, which is one of the beauties of the true Poodle. Also the nails must be kept short, so that the Poodle can walk high on his pads. If his nails are long they will "click" on the floor and then push the foot back on the pastern, giving the Poodle a flat and ungainly foot instead of the well-arched, well muscled-up foot which is correct. For the perfect foot of the show dog, you will do well to file back the nails after cutting them. This should be done when the Poodle has just been bathed and the nails are then soft. The best instrument for this is the smallest type of cross-cut carpenter's file—a file about 4in. long and ½in. wide, tapering at the end.

In the early summer, wasp stings are a danger, especially to dogs' feet and mouths, as they so often paw at the wasp or snap at it. It is advisable to keep a bottle of lotion ready made up, of one teaspoonful bicarbonate of soda to ten ounces of water. Dab this on the sting freely, even if in the mouth, for about five minutes without stopping and it will greatly help. An even simpler remedy is to rub the place of the sting with a piece of ordinary washing soda.

Anal glands will also need attention from time to time. These are two glands at the entrance to the rectum which secrete a certain amount of rather evil smelling fluid, and the ducts need to be squeezed out regularly. We do this small, but rather unpleasant job, three times a year. If your Poodle is inclined to lick round his tail, or scrub his back parts along on the ground, it is usually a sign that his anal glands need attention, and you would be advised to call in the vet. to attend to this until you have learned to cope with it yourself.

Puppies, like children, do from time to time, suffer from upset tummies, and billious attacks, but with a little attention at the first sign these slight indispositions pass quickly. Keep your Poodle warm and quiet, and do not give him anything to eat for twenty-four hours. This period of starvation will do him the world of good and he will come back on his food with added vigour. If he is vomiting, make up a mixture of the *white* only of a raw egg, one teaspoonful of glucose and a tablespoonful of cold water that has been boiled. Give a *teaspoonful* of this mixture every two hours, and unless the sickness is the forerunner of some more serious ailment you will find your Poodle is quickly his normal self again.

Poodles are a most hardy and healthy breed, and given ordinary normal attention and good quality food, they usually lead a very trouble-free and healthy life. Skin diseases are rare in the Poodle, and they are by no means delicate in either digestion or chest.

So now we will assume that your Poodle puppy has got through his baby troubles and is all set for his adult life.

5

TRAINING THE POODLE

House Training—Lead Training—Show Training.

The initial training of a young Poodle puppy is the same, whether it is to be a delightful companion or a potential show winner.

First and foremost it has to fit into your home life, and this is a big undertaking for a small bundle of fluff and mischief aged only eight weeks. Think for a moment of your puppy's previous existence; he, or she, has probably been kept in a kennel and run with several others; there is nothing to bump into such as chair or table legs, no slippery polished floors, and above all no carpets that must not have puddles, or worse, made on them; again, there are no humans marching round with large feet that always manage to tread on small paws. Life is quite an ordered affair, meals shared with others are a delightful scrimmage; who can eat fastest gets most; no-one disturbs one's rest unless it is a fellow pup who nestles beside one. Now everything is strange and terrifying, commencing with a journey by car or train which usually makes you sick because you are not used to it; then there are masses of loud-voiced humans who drag you around and try to make you play, and wherever you walk you bump into something; overcome by all this you make a puddle on the carpet and are promptly told you are a bad, dirty pup. Bed-time comes, and after all the petting and playing you are left alone in a dark room. You get out of your basket in search of your brothers and sisters and lose yourself in the unfamiliar surroundings; in your misery you lift your nose in the air and howl for comfort and wish you were back in your nice warm kennel, and so undoubtedly do all the other occupants of the house!

Well, we have drawn this picture to make you see the puppy's point of view, but none of this need happen if you are careful. Remembering how strange your puppy feels and how easily he gets tired, give him a warm drink when he arrives, with a little glucose or honey in it and do not give him his proper meal for an hour or two. Have prepared a good deep box *which he cannot get out of* and into this put some straw or an old blanket. Make a nest in the centre, and in this place a stone or metal hot water bottle. Your puppy does not need this to keep him warm but to supply the cosiness of his missing companions for the first night or two. Allow him to have a good romp before finally going to bed, then put the hot water bottle under the bedding and pop him in with a biscuit or bone to chew. Nearly cover the opening of the box with a light blanket or sack and leave him finally in the dark. He will probably cry or even yell for a short while, but he is nice and warm, his tummy is full and sleep will soon quieten him, and everyone should have a good and peaceful night.

Now comes the job of training, and the greatest thing to remember is always try to *avoid* a battle of wills. You cannot for instance *force* your puppy to walk on a lead if he makes up his mind not to do so, and to give him *his* way spells constant future trouble.

House Training is your first task, and this can be quite quickly done if you are prepared to work really hard at it for a few days. Never forget that a young puppy has little or no control over his bodily functions; often he does not even know that he wants to make a puddle until the harm is done, and he cannot possibly understand that it is not *what* he has done but *where* he has done it that brings forth the cross voice and hard slap. No, if your pup makes puddles or worse on your carpets during his first week or two, you must blame yourself and not him. Here is a simple method: select a suitable spot in your garden, and after every time you feed him and whenever he wakes from sleep take him to this spot. At first he will try your patience nearly to breaking point by playing, but soon he will realize what he is there for. As soon as he has obliged, give him a small titbit as a reward, and take him straight in again. This is important, as it teaches him to be quick, a useful habit when you are in a hurry to go out. It is quite useless to put the pup out after he has made the puddle on the carpet, his little brain can see no possible connection; you must just be quicker next time.

Training to stay alone. The easiest way to teach this very

PLATE I. An example of five generations of line breeding, showing how similarity of type has been achieved. *Photo: H. G. Goater*

PLATE II. A promising pair of young Toy Poodles. *Photo: Margaret Worth*

PLATE III. The Poodle ring at one of the Championship Shows giving a good example of ringcraft and handling.

Photo: Margaret Worth

PLATE IV. A group of Rothara stud dogs; left to right: Rothara Wychwood the Spark, Rothara the Berkshire Lad, Rothara the Little Bogey, Rothara Piccoli Merry Quip, Rothara the Tympany of Tusette, Rothara the Black Buccaneer and Rothara the Roysterer.

Photo: Fall

useful virtue is always to put your pup in his box for half
an hour to an hour after his meals; a habit is soon formed.
Whenever I have a young pup in the house I provide it with
a "toy box"; a small carton is useful and into this I put such
things as an old nylon stocking knotted, a small ball, a couple
of bones, an old shoe or glove, an empty sugar packet, etc.
When I want to leave the pup alone I give him his "toy box"
and leave him to unpack it. This will keep him quiet for quite
a while. When his time alone is over, pack up the toys and
remove the box; remember that it must be a treat to have it.
The best time to be alone is after a meal.

Training to walk on a lead. After your pup has been with you
a few days and has settled down, it is time to start lead
training. To commence, get him to follow you wherever you
go in the house and garden; call him to you and get him to
walk close behind you; when he does this nicely, put a small
collar on him for several short periods during the day, and
again encourage him to follow you; whenever you put the
collar on always say "walkies", or some such word. Don't
leave the collar on for more than fifteen minutes at a time and
always give a reward before taking it off. The next step is to
attach a light lead to the collar, and again encourage him to
follow you with the lead trailing on the ground; he will be
a little bothered at first, but will soon get used to it. Give him
plenty of encouragement and praise. When he has become
used to the lead, carry him to the end of the path or lawn, put
him down and holding the end of the lead quite slackly
encourage him to walk *back* to the house. Repeat this a time
or two, always walking *towards* the house and giving a reward
on reaching it. In a few days you will find he will walk quite
steadily beside you. Train your puppy to walk on either side
of you not on one side only. Show dogs have to walk on one's
left, but it is useful if they will walk on the right as well.

Training to stay tied up. There may come a time when for some
reason it is essential for your dog to be tied up in a certain
place, even though he is not a show dog, so it is useful to add
this to your early training, and it is an easy matter if
approached in the right way. Put on your pup's collar and
lead, and taking his usual sleeping rug from his box, attach

his lead to the leg of a firm table or chair in the room in which you are going to be working. We usually use the kitchen table while we are cooking or washing up; put the rug on the floor, place the pup on it and say firmly "stay". Of course he will not understand at first and will probably make quite a fuss, but don't give in, just talk to him while you continue to work. Five minutes is long enough the first time, and don't forget the reward at the end. Continue the training every day, making the period longer each time, and making a point of going in and out of the room, gradually leaving him for longer and longer; as long as he has the security of his blanket he will not be afraid. You must, of course, on no account leave a tied up puppy alone in the house, and never leave a lead on a dog in a car, as it may easily hang itself.

Training for the Show Ring. We like to start this training very early in life. If you have bred the puppy yourself you can start putting him up on a table as early as six weeks old, and by twelve weeks he will probably be walking well on a lead. We have proved from long experience that the earlier you start training a show puppy the easier it comes for both puppy and trainer and the better the results, and we think that the exhibitor who brings a rather unruly and unwilling youngster of eight or nine months old into the ring and says, "he never had a lead on till yesterday", has nothing to be proud of but is just admitting lack of preparation. The well-trained puppy should walk proudly in the ring knowing just what is expected of him, and be full of confidence in himself and his owner. Most puppies love training and regard it as a game full of good rewards. If you intend to show, train your puppy well.

We would strongly advise you to go to a Dog Show as soon as possible and watch exactly what happens; the experience you will gain by watching both the judge and the handlers, plus the instruction in this book, should enable you to do the job competently.

Your most important object is to accustom your pup to all the different things which happen at a show, so that he is forewarned and his confidence will not be shaken.

Having got your puppy walking nicely on the lead, start training to show walk. Just mark out a short distance in your garden on lawn or path, or if winter time, in your hall or passage, placing a table at one end. It is essential to make the space fairly small as your puppy will always walk well if the show ring is larger than he is used to at home, but if he is trained to a very large space and then is shown in a cramped ring he may be upset by it.

First walk your puppy round your imaginary ring on your *left* side, the dog being on the *inside* of the circle; hold the end of the lead in your right hand and take up the slack with your left. Walk smartly, keeping the puppy's head well up, and gradually, as training proceeds, slacken the lead until he walks nicely on his own.

Now for training to be handled on a table: So many unpleasant things happen on a table—grooming, dosing, clipping, etc., that it is essential that you should get this table business associated with something pleasant in his mind, and the easiest way to do this is to give him his meals on a table. First of all be sure the table is steady; nothing terrifies a young animal more than to feel the ground, i.e. table, rocking under him; if the surface is polished and slippery, cover it with a rug or sack, or small rubber mat. When dinner-time comes round show the dish to the pup and then lift him up on to the table and hold the dish under his chin. Do not worry about the way he stands for the first time or two. When he has quite got used to eating on the table, hold the dish in your left hand, and with your right hand put his hind legs in place and stroke his tail into an upright position. You should also practice this on the floor.

When your pup has quite got his confidence on the table, it is time to start getting him used to being handled. Therefore feel all over his neck and head and measure his ears along his nose; the judge will ask to see his mouth and by this he means his teeth. He does not want the mouth opened. Very gently take hold of the upper lip on either side of his jaws and pull the lips back revealing the teeth, and at the same time pull down the lower lip with the other hand. This must be done gently or your pup may become difficult and resist his mouth being looked at in the judging, which may cost him a prize. Continuing down his fore-legs pick up his feet and feel the pads, then run your hands over his shoulders along his flanks, over his hind-quarters, under his tail and down his hind legs; then place your hand on his quarters and give a gentle press.

Your pup must learn to resist this pressure and not sit down. Practice these same movements on the floor so that he is not afraid to have someone standing over him. If you go through these actions daily, your puppy will soon have all the confidence in the world and be a model of good show behaviour. Remember that your job as a trainer is to accustom your dog to everything that is expected of him *before* he goes into the ring at his first show. Incidentally, it is quite in order for you to speak quietly to your dog whilst the judge is handling him, but you must never call him by his registered name; many novice handlers make this error, the old hands, of course, know that it just isn't done.

6

CARE OF THE POODLE COAT

Grooming—Coat Changing—Bathing and Drying.

MANY people are doubtful of owning a Poodle because they are worried about the time they will have to spend looking after its coat, but these stories you have heard of having to spend endless time every day brushing and combing are just a lot of exaggeration. Of course your Poodle's coat needs looking after if he is to stay well and clean and look smart, but luckily you can limit the amount of work you have to do by the kind of clip in which you decide to keep him.

Most people buy a Poodle between two and three months of age—under eight weeks is too young for a puppy to leave it's first home surroundings unless you are very expert at Poodle rearing—and if you buy one over three to three-and-a-half months it will already have started to form habits, some of which may be bad ones.

Your twelve weeks' old puppy should have a coat $1\frac{1}{2}$in. to 2in. in length and should, before it is handed over to you, have had its face, feet and tail neatly clipped; you can have a moustache or not, as you like. This puppy coat will probably not be very curly and you should just brush and comb it through every day. The best comb to buy is a steel one which has quite widely-spaced teeth one end and much finer the other. You should use the coarse end for the body and legs, and the fine end for the head, ears and tail. Many puppies are rather naughty about being groomed, so start on the job when he is tired, or just had a good meal. Lie him on your knee, head towards your chest, and comb steadily first one side and then the other, then down his chest, under his fore legs and up inside his back legs; then let him sit up, and do down the centre of his back, and finally his head, ears and tail. He will probably object with all his small strength at first, but stand no nonsense and he will soon learn that the quieter he is the sooner the horrid business will be over. As he grows older and more sensible you can get him to lie on a table.

If your puppy's coat begins to get rather long and straggly it probably needs "tipping". To "tip" a puppy's coat, comb the hair upwards, and with your scissors cut off about half an inch of coat evenly all over, getting the finished result as level as possible. It will be found that this adds strength to the coat, and a thick and springy texture will grow by the time you wish to put him into his first proper clip. When he or she is between six and eight months old it is time to decide upon the style of clip you want. (See Chapter 7).

Between the ages of twelve and fifteen months, your Poodle will cast his puppy coat; you may have been told that Poodles are different to other dogs—"they never cast their coats". Of course every dog changes coat, but because of their curly coat the dead hair, when it comes away from the skin, remains in the coat instead of falling on the carpet. This is what causes mats, and if the Poodle is bathed *before* this dead hair is removed by combing, the result will be a solid felt mat all over the body close to the skin. Once this happens there is nothing to be done but to cut off the coat and let it grow again.

If you regularly groom your young Poodle a minimum of twice a week you will soon notice, when the change of coat starts to take place, small loose knots appear often no bigger than a pin's head. This is your danger signal, and for the next ten days or so you must somehow find time to brush and comb your Poodle *right down* to *the skin, every day*. Once this period is over and your Poodle has got rid of his baby coat, you will only need to give him a quick brush over to smarten him up when you wish to take him out, and a really good "down to the skin" combing once a week. Even our top show Poodles are only groomed once a week once they have their adult coats.

It is said that constant washing ruins both human and canine hair; and this again I think is a falacy providing you take precautions to put back into the coat the natural oil the washing has removed. With your own hair you probably use a cream rinse to finish off your shampoo. With a Poodle you should use a conditioning cream or coat corrector. Above all, do use a *soapless shampoo*. Human shampoos are inclined to soften the coat too much, and some brands of canine shampoos, whilst good for harsher-coated dogs, tend to strip the natural oil from the Poodle coat and cause it to break off at half its

CARE OF THE POODLE COAT

natural length. "Vitacoat" supply various excellent shampoos especially adapted for all colours of Poodles, and also a Lanoline cream rinse which does keep the coat in good condition.

Having groomed your dog first, prepare everything you need for the bath; two towels, a suitable table in front of a fire or heater, a hair dryer if you have one, your jug of ready mixed shampoo and a clean brush and comb. It is most important that no water should enter the ears, so place little swabs of cotton wool dipped in vaseline or pure face cream in each ear, gently pushing it well down with your little finger. Also put a smear of the same ointment all round his eyes, then pop him into the sink in which you have about 3in. of warm water and start to get him wet, either using a hand spray or a small jug. Commence shampooing him at the head; be very careful it does not run over into his eyes. Wash his head, neck, ears (especially underneath), down his chest and between his front legs, continue down his back and under his tummy, then his front legs and feet, paying special attention to his elbows, down his back, hind legs and his tail. Rinse him in the same way, being sure his head, ears and back are clean before you tackle his sides and legs. When all shampoo is rinsed off take a little condition cream on your hand, rub your hands together, then massage well into the coat; rinse off in the same way. Let him have a good shake, then wrap him up in a nice warm towel while you dry his face and underparts and remove the swabs from his ears. Dry off his coat either with a hair dryer or by brushing him continuously in front of a fire. Comb him out just *before* he is quite dry, give him a final dry off and then put him in a warm place to rest for an hour or so. Be very careful that he does not go out and catch cold or be left to sleep in a draughty place.

If you follow the above directions carefully, and especially if you train your Poodle right from the first to lie quietly while being groomed, you will have a dog who will do you great credit and of whom you can be justly proud.

7

POODLE CLIPPING

Puppy Clip—Lamb or Curly Clip—Dutch or Modern Clip—Lion or Traditional Clip—Continental Clip.

As you have chosen the Poodle as the breed of dog you wish to own, you will naturally have realized beforehand that you will have to spend quite a lot of time in clipping your Poodle and keeping him in a smart condition. Most Poodles are temperamentally co-operative over their appearance and seem to take a great delight in being groomed. There is no doubt that they are extremely vain. The clipping of a Poodle may appear difficult, and although at first the results of your labours may not be very professional, with practice you will very soon learn to turn out your Poodle reasonably well. If you can get an expert to show you exactly *how* to do it, you will save yourself a lot of trouble; but if that is impossible there is no reason at all why you should not learn to keep your Poodle in excellent trim, from illustrations.

There are five different styles for a Poodle, and you will decide which appeals to you most. These are (1) Puppy Clip, (2) Lamb or Curly Clip, (3) Dutch or Modern Clip, (4) Lion Clip, (5) Continental Clip.

Most Poodle owners keep their Poodles in Puppy Clip until they reach the age of six or eight months. If you have it in mind to show your Poodle, you will probably decide to put him into Lion Clip at about nine months old. If, however, you have no thought of showing your Poodle, the best clip for him is either the Dutch or Modern Clip or the Lamb Clip.

THE PUPPY CLIP (Fig. 1): This is the first stage in the clipping of a Poodle, and for this the hair is closely clipped from the face, feet and tail only. The rest of the hair on the body is left at the existing length. When clipping your puppy in this style a line should be taken from the corner of the eye to the opening of the ear, and then down to the middle of the throat. Never cut away the hair *above* the eyes. The feet should be

FIG. 1. PUPPY CLIP

clipped up to just *below* the ankle joint on both front and back feet. The tail should be clipped from the root to about halfway along the tail, leaving a good thick "pom" of hair on the end. Some puppies are rather naughty about being clipped to begin with and if you yourself are not very expert at the job you may prefer to start your trimming operations with scissors only and leave the wielding of clippers until a little later on. A very good finish can be obtained by using scissors only.

THE LAMB OR CURLY CLIP (Fig. 2) is a very popular clip and very workmanlike. It is a good country trim. It is really a shorter variation of the Puppy Trim. In this, the face, feet and tail are clipped but the hair on the body is cut much shorter than in the Puppy Clip. A moustache may be left on the muzzle, or the Poodle can be clean shaven. The tail can retain the "pom" or the hair can be cut short leaving just a stump.

THE DUTCH OR MODERN CLIP (Fig. 3) is a more fancy style and is seen a great deal in London and the big towns. Here, the hair on the front and hind legs, including the shoulders

FIG. 2. CURLY CLIP

and the hips is cut to a length of about 1½in., and is often likened to "cowboy trousers". The hair on the body and neck is cut very short, while the face, feet and tail are again clipped. In this style, a moustache can be left if desired, and the hair on the top of the head is rounded off and of a moderate length. A "pom" is left on the tail.

THE LION CLIP (Fig. 4), which is generally accepted as the traditional show clip, is the exact opposite of the Dutch Clip, in that here the hair on the front legs is clipped short from the ankle to the elbow, leaving a rounded "bracelet" of hair on the actual wrist joint with the feet clipped short. A "mane" of hair is left on the shoulders, neck and body down to the lowest rib bone, and this mane grows to a length of at least 5in. when the Poodle is mature. The hair on the hindquarters is cut moderately short to a length of about ¾in. to 1in., and two rings are clipped on the hind legs, leaving a rounded bracelet of rather longer hair which covers the back ankle and the knee joint. The face, feet and tail are again closely clipped and no moustache is left. A generous "pom" is left on the tail, and the top-knot is allowed to grow moderately long and is usually tied up with a bow to keep the hair out of the eyes. There are quite a number of variations in the Lion Clip and these usually take the form of rings, rosettes or

POODLE CLIPPING 41

Fig. 3. DUTCH CLIP

Fig. 4. LION CLIP

FIG. 5. CONTINENTAL CLIP

saddles clipped into the short hair on the lower part of the back where the mane ends.

THE CONTINENTAL CLIP (Fig. 5) is a variation of the Lion Clip, and in this clip the mane is kept but the top-knot is shorter and rounded and is not usually tied in a ribbon. The hair from the end of the mane down to the bracelet on the back ankle is clipped close the same length as the face, feet and tail. A "pom" is left on the tail, bracelets on the front legs, and a very small "French" looking moustache is left on the upper part of the muzzle; there is no beard of any kind on the lower jaws. Again, rings and rosettes of various patterns may be fashioned on the lower back and hips as desired.

There is much argument as to which is the most attractive clip. It may probably safely be said that the Lion Clip is the most elegant and probably gives the vital joints and organs of the Poodle more protection from cold and rain; but on the other hand the Dutch Clip can look extremely smart and jaunty. On the whole the Lion Clip is easier to keep in good fettle and certainly a Poodle gets far less muddy and wet in the winter with his shaven legs, than the Poodle in Modern Clip who gets most bedraggled and sodden in snowy and wet weather. A Poodle's coat is extremely waterproof and it takes a very wet day for the rain to get down to his skin. Usually a shake is enough and the hair underneath the top layer remains quite dry.

It has been said that Poodles are an expensive luxury because they need frequent visits to the Beauty Parlour for clipping every few weeks, but this need not be so. If you start clipping your Poodle at an early age and do this often, you will find you can very soon turn him out to look extremely smart. At first he may look somewhat shaggy and not quite what you hoped, but after a little practice you will find that you are becoming adept at the art. If possible, try to take a few lessons from someone who clips well, or else take your Poodle to a canine Beauty Parlour and ask if you may watch while he is being clipped. You can learn a lot this way, and once the "line" of the clip you have chosen is there, you will not find it difficult to maintain him in this smart condition.

For equipment, you will need a good sharp pair of scissors— hair-dressing type—if possible. You will also need a pair of hand clippers, size 00. When you have become adept at using hand clippers, and perhaps when you have more than one poodle, you may decide to purchase a pair of electric clippers, of which there are quite a few on the market. Electric clippers are not difficult to use, and provided they are kept well oiled and the teeth well brushed out after each time of using, they are worth the extra expense. Most Poodles take to them kindly and they certainly give a better finish and are, of course, very much quicker to use than hand clippers. But it is essential to oil them before and after use, and also to brush all hairs from between the blades before putting them away.

8

POODLE BREEDING

Management of the Stud Dog—Choice of the Stud Dog—Care of the Brood Bitch—Mating of the Bitch.

IF you have decided to put your Poodle dog at stud, or breed from your Poodle bitch, there are quite a number of points to be considered beforehand. Let us assume that you have decided, now your Poodle dog is a year old, that you are going to place him at stud. The first step is to "prove" him, and to do this it is usual to use him on one of your own bitches, or alternatively to offer his stud service free of charge to ascertain that he is capable of siring a litter. In this case choose an older bitch if possible which has already had a litter. The owner of the bitch may agree to give you one of the puppies free of charge if a litter results. You should not put your dog at public stud until he has to your certain knowledge sired a litter.

Assuming that all goes well and your Poodle is a proved sire, the next step is to advertise him either locally or in the canine journals, stating his breeding, colour, age and the fee you have decided to charge. If it is possible to enter him at various shows, and if he has won some prizes you will find that this will increase the demand for him at stud. As you now intend to take money for his services, there are certain obligations attached to this. First of all, he must be kept scrupulously clean at all times, free from any pests of any kind, in really good condition, and in a smart clip. He must be ready for inspection at a moment's notice and always looking his best. But above all, you must not plan to put him at stud unless he is a really sound dog, sound in his action, and correct in his conformation. He should not be placed at stud if he has any glaring faults that he could pass on to his progeny. If you are quite satisfied on this latter point, you will probably find he is quite in demand and will have several bookings and then he will need extra food such as raw eggs and milk, plenty of good quality meat, and he will also need plenty of good hard exercise.

POODLE BREEDING

As he is now placed at stud it is not enough to put him alone with the bitch when she arrives for the mating. You will need to learn how to assist him, and guard against any mishap once he and bitch are "tied". The "tieing" process lasts for anything between five minutes and fifty-five minutes, and during this time the dog and bitch are unable to get away from each other. Occasionally the bitch may be a little excitable and unless restrained may injure both herself and the dog. So you should not leave them alone until the mating is absolutely completed and during this time you should keep a restraining hand on both of them to prevent any damage.

When the mating is over the dog should be made to rest quietly by himself in his usual bed for at least two or three hours. He should not be fed for two hours either before or after the stud, and he should be given every opportunity to relieve himself just before he is introduced to the bitch.

It is usual for the stud fee to be paid at the time of the mating, and in return a copy of the dog's pedigree should be handed to the owner of the bitch, together with a certificate of mating, the date she is due to whelp, and a receipt for the stud fee.

The Choice of the Stud Dog

If on the other hand, you own the bitch and have decided to mate her at her next season, you will want to be sure that you have chosen the right dog. What memories of discussions and cogitations this invokes for many of us who have been breeding for a number of years! I sometimes wonder if we owners of several well known sires do not perhaps forget how important this choice is to the owner of the single much-loved little bitch, and I also wonder if the owners of bitches fully realize their great responsibility to the Poodle as a breed, whatever its size, and that it lies very largely in *their hands* whether Poodles shall continue in the future to be the charming, gay, intelligent dogs with sound action and carrying coats of the many beautiful single colours or whether they will degenerate into nasty, snappy, timid little horrors with unsound limbs and mis-marked parti-coloured coats, light coloured eyes and wrongly placed teeth and who are shy of strangers even in their own home surroundings. Such dogs are a pleasure to no-one. The owners of the well-known kennels and many of the smaller ones are doing their best to improve the breed in spite of its dangerous popularity, but unless we are going to receive the intelligent co-operation of the countless owners of pet Poodles, all our efforts will be of no avail.

Firstly, let me correct a widely held belief, namely, that the dog has more effect on the resultant litter than the bitch. This is not true except in an infinitesimal number of cases. Very occasionally over a period of years, there arises a dog who is so dominant in himself that he stamps all his progeny. This is what is known as a prepotent sire and amongst these few are the great dogs of the breed and their names will be found behind literally hundreds of present-day dogs. But believe me such dogs are very few and far between. The owner of such a dog will guard it with the utmost care and the sentence which appears on most stud cards "to approved bitches only" really means something in his case.

Now, let us consider your bitch impartially and without rose coloured spectacles! She probably falls into one of the following categories:—

1. The well-bred show quality bitch.
2. The well-bred bitch with a certain definite fault or faults.
3. The bitch which is a fair specimen but which is not particularly well bred, i.e. no really first-class dogs or bitches' names appear amongst her parents or grandparents' names on her pedigree.
4. The bitch which has been bought very cheaply as a pet only, which has several serious faults and whose pedigree, if she has one, should have been endorsed by her breeder as "Unfit for breeding".

The category 1. bitch presents an easy task when deciding on a suitable stud dog, for providing that you got her from a reliable breeder whom you can trust and whose stud dogs are not only big winners themselves but also the consistent begetters of top quality progeny of perfect temperament, you cannot do better than take his or her advice as to which dog is the most suitable mate for your bitch.

If your bitch comes under category number 2, as is the case when a very promising puppy develops an unsuspected fault as she grows up, again you would be wise to follow the same advice as in category 1, as the trustworthy breeder will be as anxious as you are to correct this unexpected fault which has developed in your bitch, from passing on to her progeny. If, however, you have unknowingly purchased an adult or near adult with a pronounced fault or have been told by an unscrupulous breeder that a fault "does not matter" or "will come right", you would be wise to seek for your stud dog elsewhere than in the original kennel, in order to overcome this fault as speedily as possible.

If you find yourself in this latter situation, you will probably be wise to mate your bitch to a dog who is a complete or partial "outcross", i.e. a Poodle who carries either no similar names to your bitch in his pedigree or only in his grandparents or great-grandparents.

In order to get such a mate for your bitch, you should get in touch with the owner of the top Poodle kennel in your colour, i.e. black if she is black, white if she is white or cream, silver if she is silver, brown if she is brown. Most famous kennels, while possessing stud dogs of different colours, are generally renowned for one particular colour in which they have established, or are on the way to establishing, a "line". The dogs in such kennels will have been most carefully linebred for many generations and will, if originally based on good stock, have produced a "type", so that each succeeding generation, though better than the previous one in the finer points, resembles it so closely that the owner often finds it quite difficult to quickly distinguish between father and son, mother and daughter, etc. If the dogs from such kennels are not only consistent winners themselves, but their progeny are good winners in other hands, you may be sure that the "type" is a good one.

Once you have decided into which "line" you wish to mate your bitch, you should seek the advice of the owner, frankly stating your reason for wishing to mate into that line and clearly stating the fault you are hoping to correct. The breeder will probably not consent to your using his or her best dog but will agree to mate your bitch to a close relation of the dog who does not carry your bitch's fault.

Should you get a bitch puppy without this fault from the resulting litter, you would do well to keep it and mate back again into the chosen line. If you continue to mate each succeeding generation into this famous line, your original faulty stock will become gradually strengthened with sound stock until it is so strong that you will have virtually changed your line of breeding, altered your type to the one you admire and be as safe as it is possible to be in nature, from the original fault.

Category 3 presents a different problem and here you have little to guide you as to the best direction to take. A safe rule to follow in such a case is to mate your bitch to the best type you can in your colour providing he carries none of her faults. In other words "like to like in all their respective virtues but never in their respective faults". *Never lose sight of the fact that a nervous temperament is a most serious fault in any breed of dog and the one that will most quickly make that breed unpopular with the general public.* It is also one of the most difficult faults to breed out. Therefore beware of the stud dog who refuses to be friendly or which you are not allowed to touch when you visit his owner's kennel. "Don't touch" notices above a dog's bench at a show are an entirely different matter and are merely to protect the dog from disease and from dirty hands. The owner will always get the dog out of its bench for you to see and handle, if you ask.

With category 4 the case is clear and heartbreaking. Heartless as it may appear, the only honest thing you can do is never to breed from such a bitch. Let her, in spite of all her faults, remain your close companion and beloved friend but for the sake of the whole breed of Poodles don't *you* be responsible for the production of such a litter of puppies, themselves potential breeders of bad stock. If you *must*, for any health reasons breed from such a bitch, again *be honest* and sell the resultant puppies cheaply *without a pedigree.*

Finally to all owners of Poodle bitches whatever their size I would say this—You are the owner of an animal belonging to one of the finest, healthiest, most intelligent and elegant breeds of dogs in Britain to-day. *Make it your proud boast that you have done everything in your power to breed a better Poodle than the one you possess.*

Having borne in mind all the above points and chosen the stud dog you fancy, write or telephone the owner and make a provisional booking for the near future, saying when your bitch is expected in season. When she actually comes in season, immediately get in touch with the owner of the stud dog and make a definite appointment for the mating on the 10th, 11th or 12th day of her season. Before arriving for the mating, you must ensure that the bitch is quite clean in coat and skin, well groomed and in perfect health in every way. She should not have been fed within three hours of mating and should have been given ample opportunity of relieving herself before being put with the dog. Most owners of stud dogs prefer to take the bitch away to mate quietly with the stud dog without the presence of strangers, and undoubtedly nearly all bitches behave much better under these circumstances. However, you should ask to see the dog you have chosen before the mating, and also again ask to be taken to your bitch when the two are safely "tied". For one thing the bitch will like to have you there at that time to hold her and reassure her, and also you will naturally wish to check that the chosen stud dog has in fact been used. After the mating has been completed, the bitch should not be allowed to relieve herself, unless absolutely necessary for about one hour and she should rest for some time if possible, and by that is meant no hard running or walking exercise.

If you find you cannot take your bitch personally to be mated and have to send her by train, there are one or two points to be borne in mind. Firstly, make it quite clear which dog you wish to use. Make very definite arrangements with the owner of the stud dog as to the station to which the bitch is to be sent, and the actual time of arrival, and send the bitch in a strong, safe travelling box marked "To be Called For" and "Bitch in season, please do not let out". If possible also mark the label with the stud dog owner's telephone number. Don't forget to include the return carriage in your remittance for the stud fee, and do remember to mention the pet name of your bitch.

After all these points have been carefully dealt with, it is now a matter of being patient and waiting for the litter to arrive. Do remember to write at once and inform the owner of the stud dog the result of the mating. This information is much appreciated, not only because very careful records are kept but also because a great personal interest will almost certainly have been taken. If by any chance the bitch should fail to produce a litter, then the stud dog owner should be notified within seven days of the expected date and if a free mating at the next season is required, a vet's certificate is advisable to corroborate the fact that there have been no puppies this time. Most owners will be quite willing to give one free service at the next season if no puppies have materialized, provided the same stud dog is still in their possession, although it is not incumbent upon them to do so. It is as well to enquire into this point when mating the bitch. If your bitch has missed you should not ask for the free use of another stud dog belonging to the owner, nor should you ask to bring a different bitch. The stud dog is a reliable proved sire, and will presumably have sired quite a number of litters. Therefore it is reasonable to expect that as he has completed his side of the bargain, the fault probably lies with the bitch rather than the dog. The size of the litter lies entirely with the bitch, since the dog at a single ejection releases a large number of sperm, but the bitch sends down only a small number of eggs to become fertilized by the dog. Some bitches are only in a suitable condition for conceiving a litter for a matter of a few hours, but the majority of bitches are absolutely ready for mating between the tenth and thirteenth days of the season at the very least. Some can even be mated as late as the twenty-first day, but this is not usual.

Should your bitch get out and become mated with an undesirable dog, it is possible for her to have an injection from the Veterinary Surgeon which will nullify the mating. This injection must be given before 36 hours have passed since she mated with the undesirable dog and is almost always effective. This injection prolongs the actual season for another fourteen to twenty-one days, so care must be taken to keep the bitch under safe control for this extra time. She can be mated with the right dog during this second period if desired, and although it is rather doubtful that a litter will result, it sometimes does and is worth trying if a litter is absolutely essential at this particular season.

9

THE FIRST POODLE LITTER

Whelping Quarters—Pre-whelping Preparation and Care of the Bitch—
Birth of the Puppies—Weaning.

Your Poodle bitch has now been safely and satisfactorily mated to the dog of your selection, and there is little to do but wait patiently for the resulting litter of puppies. The period of gestation for a bitch is sixty-two days, but quite often a first litter may arrive three or four days early. Poodles are, on the whole, extremely easy and sensible whelpers and there are seldom any complications provided they have been well fed and well exercised during their pregnancy. We make a practice of giving the bitch a worm dose ten days after the mating, as we have found that this does ensure that the puppies are born comparatively free of worms and remain free throughout their early puppyhood.

Whelping Quarters. The place in which your bitch is going to whelp needs consideration, and if this is well planned in advance you will be able to get her to take kindly to the place you have in mind rather than the most unsuitable place that takes her fancy. In this establishment we have found that a small indoor kennel is the most satisfactory, and in the accompanying illustration (Fig. 6) you will find a recommended design.

This kennel is made of a light wood with a door opening at the front for easy cleaning; but more important, a door that also hinges back on the top so that easy inspection of the puppies can be made without disturbing them. This kennel is made by Messrs. E. F. Hare & Sons Ltd., of Market Deeping, Lincs., in varying sizes and is extremely reasonable in price. An electric stove can be placed near, and the heat will penetrate easily through the front bars and give the family plenty of warmth. The bitch should be introduced to this kennel a good fortnight before she is due to whelp, and gradually shut in for

FIG. 6.

Whelping Box standing on 3" legs to facilitate access of the bitch.

very short periods at a time, preferably being given a bone or a favourite meal in the kennel so that she associates the quarters with pleasure. Very soon she will feel quite at home in this kennel and will of her own accord sleep in it for the last week if she has her own particular rug. It should be left open in the daytime so that she can get into it whenever she likes. When her puppies have safely arrived and the bitch has been tidied up, a clean blanket or sack should be nailed to the floor of the kennel, fitting close up to the walls. This will give the puppies a surface on which they can get a purchase for their little feet when feeding, and as it is fastened down, there is no chance of their getting between the folds, and thus sat on or suffocated. The blanket can easily be changed when necessary.

PRE-WHELPING PREPARATION. Six days before the bitch is due to whelp she will need a certain amount of preparation. The hair should be trimmed off closely round each nipple, and

THE FIRST POODLE LITTER

the area well washed and carefully dried. Each nipple should be gently rubbed with a little olive oil to keep it soft and supple. The hair round her back parts should be carefully trimmed away, and these parts sponged with warm water and a little T.C.P. or Milton every day to ensure that she is quite sanitary. If she has a heavy coat, it is advisable to cut this down to about 1in. or 1½in., so that it can be kept in better condition in every way. This will also ensure that instead of becoming thin and wispy when she has finished nursing her litter, it will have remained quite dense and will quickly grow to its normal length again, always providing of course that she is well fed during lactation and after.

FEEDING. With regard to feeding during pregnancy, no change is necessary until the fifth week, but at this period she will benefit by a raw egg and milk about three times a week for breakfast, and an increase in the daily amount of meat she usually eats. A very good guide to the amount of meat suitable for a dog, is half an ounce of meat to every pound body weight, but the proportion to body weight should be increased in special circumstances such as when a stud dog has a full engagement list, or when a bitch is pregnant, or when dogs are being specially conditioned for the show ring.

When the bitch comes to the beginning of the seventh week of her pregnancy, her daily food content should be divided into more meals per day so that her stomach is never overloaded nor uncomfortable. A good working time-table at this stage is:—*Breakfast:* A drink of honey and milk, or a raw egg and milk. *Dinner:* Raw or cooked meat. *Supper:* Raw or cooked meat again, or liver or fish mixed with a good quality biscuit soaked in stock or gravy. This diet can be continued right up until the time of whelping, but care should be taken that the bitch neither gains too much fat (although her weight will materially increase because of the presence of the puppies) nor becomes in any way thin or "ribby". She should have clean fresh water easily accessible to her at all times. As soon as she has produced her puppies her diet should be altered completely for the first two or three days. A really excellent food for nursing bitches, and indeed for actually weening the puppies, is made as follows:- Get a packet of "Casilan" (a milk powder protein which was used, I understand, for the rehabilitation of Belsen children), two packets of "Farex" and half a packet of "Glucodin", all made by Glaxo. Mix these three powders together in a tin. For every feed of your bitch, add two desertspoonsful of the mixed powder to a quarter of a pint of warm milk and water. Stir the powder well into the milk with a fork until it is of a smooth and slightly thickened consistency. As soon as the bitch has completed her whelping, she should have a good drink of this, and then be left alone to sleep and recover from her efforts. During the first twenty-four hours after the births, she should have warm drinks of the above at intervals of three hours. After that she may have a raw egg and milk for one meal and Casilan drinks for the other meals.

On the third day she can have a meal of good quality fresh *raw* meat in addition to the egg and milk, and her two Casilan drinks. This diet can then be continued, but add a second meat meal and drop one of the drinks until the puppies are weaned. Then you will want to reduce her intake of liquids, but still feed her up well on meat and raw eggs to replace all that she has given out to her puppies.

When a bitch has completed the nursing of her puppies there is no reason at all why her condition should not be solid, and her bones well covered. If she is thin and nervy at the end of bringing up her family it means that she has not had enough meals, or the meals she has had have not been of sufficiently good quality. After all, a good price is commanded for Poodle puppies and it is absolutely incumbent upon owners to ensure that the bitch has the best and most nourishing food in return for rearing a nice litter of puppies. For three weeks before whelping and during the time she is nursing her puppies, she would benefit greatly by a daily administration of "Bemax"—a dessertspoonful over her meat daily, is the correct amount. Also it has been found that a daily dosage of "Vetzyme" tablets is excellent for the in-whelp bitch and nursing mother. An old-fashioned but very efficacious aid to a trouble-free whelping is the old gipsy remedy of Raspberry Leaf. This is always given to bitches in this kennel from halfway through pregnancy and we are proud to say that up to the time of writing there have been no casualties or difficult whelpings in this kennel. It appears that the Raspberry Leaf tablets have the effect of toning up the muscles of the womb also of producing more fluid during the actual birth of the puppies, thus obviating the pain and discomfort of "dry" births. Another excellent preparation at this time is "Sterogyl" in the form of small chocolate dragees. One tablet is given a day or so before mating, one half-way through pregnancy, and a third when the puppies are two or three days old. Each tablet contains 50,000 I.U. of Vitamin D.2 and the administration of the vitamin helps to obviate the complication of restlessness and excitability when the puppies arrive, a condition which may well develop into Eclampsia if care is not taken during pregnancy.

It should be made clear that all quantities given above refer to Miniature Poodles, and that for the larger Poodles quantities should be doubled, but for the Toy Poodles they should be halved.

EXERCISE. And now we come to one of the most essential points which help towards an easy whelping, and that is the paramount importance of regular and steady walking. The bitch should not miss a day throughout her pregnancy, even including the actual day of whelping. Of course, as her time draws near she will need shorter walks, more frequently, at a slower pace, until during the last week it will be little more than a toddle down the road and back. Always take the bitch for her exercise on a collar and lead during the second half of pregnancy. At this time she could easily be frightened by a sudden noise and rush away, or perhaps might be set on and chased by another dog. These sudden, and quite unexpected occurrences are sufficient to bring on a premature birth or cause a miscarriage, and should be avoided at all costs. At this time we must continually think ahead and give the bitch the greatest possible protection and care, for a great many of her natural defences are down and she has neither speed nor agility to combat any attack, and her instinct is to rush anywhere for safety from a foe regardless of the hazards that may be encountered on the way. Also during the latter half, the bitch will become increasingly affectionate and will rely on her owner more and more as the days go by. We are firm believers that the amount of affection, gentle handling and security that is afforded a bitch at this time, is a great factor in the degree of contentment and nice temperament of the resulting puppies. And, after all, at that time more than at any other period of her life, the bitch should have all the security and freedom from anxiety that it is within our power to give her, otherwise we are not justified in expecting her to do her part in giving valuable puppies.

THE BIRTH OF THE PUPPIES. It is advisable to acquaint your vet. with information as to the date the bitch is really due to have her puppies, and this ensures that he, or she, will be available should you need veterinary assistance. The first real sign of the approaching event is that the bitch will seem rather more affectionate and possibly "dreamy". She will undoubtedly refuse all food and drink some hours beforehand, and if you were to take her temperature you would probably find she was at least a degree and perhaps even two, below normal. We have found that plenty of newspaper in the bottom of the whelping box is helpful, as she can tear this up as much as she desires, and when the puppies arrive the paper is light and there is no danger of their suffocation from crawling into the folds. There will probably be a great deal of agitation, scratching in corners, and tearing up of any material available and the bitch will pant considerably.

There is no need to get distressed at any of these happenings, and the more she moves about in her whelping place the easier the actual whelping will probably be. She will not need you at this stage and will be completely pre-occupied with herself. But you should be around and keep a watch on her, being careful not to transmit your anxiety to the bitch. In due course she will commence her labour in earnest and you will notice that every so often she will strain, and will also note that the intervals between the bouts of straining will become less and less, while the straining itself will become more pronounced; and you will notice that what is termed the "water bag" is now protruding from the vulva. The novice may well mistake this for a puppy, but it is the mucous bag containing fluid which aids the arrival of the first puppy. You should expect the puppy to arrive quite soon after the water bag has burst, and very often the bitch herself will burst the bag by constant licking and biting. We assume that after a bigger than usual strain the first puppy pops out. Notice the time when she first begins to strain, and if she has

THE FIRST POODLE LITTER

not produced her first puppy within one to two hours, the veterinary surgeon should be called in to help matters along.

The puppies are, of course, born in a membranous sac, and most bitches will quickly tear the sac, licking and buffeting the puppy about to get the air moving freely through the lungs. She will also sever the umbilical cord by which the puppy is attached to the placenta (or after-birth). It is a disputed point whether the bitch should be allowed to eat the after-birth or whether this should quickly be taken away from her. In the wild state an animal will get rid of all trace of the birth as soon as possible so that no sign of her vulnerability shall be apparent to marauders, and also many contend that the after-birth served as nourishment for the bitch for the first twenty-four hours until she was able to hunt for food. But with domesticated animals possibly good raw meat is a better form of nourishment. If the bitch seems to have no instinct to deal with the puppy as soon as it arrives, you should promptly free it from the sac and then run your finger round the inside of the mouth to wipe away the mucous, so that it can easily breathe. The cord should then be carefully and gently severed about 3in. or 4in. from the puppy. When severing the cord be very careful not to pull *away* from the puppy's stomach—the smallest pull will cause a bad hernia. Take the cord between the first two fingers of either hand, and sever, pulling all the time *towards* the stomach. The puppy should then be rubbed quite briskly in a warm towel. This friction will cause the air to circulate in its lungs and it will become lively and quite noisy, and you will know it is safely on its way. The puppy should then be placed with the mother and she will undoubtedly attend to it.

It is not easy to be quite sure when she has had her last puppy, but usually she will turn her attention to cleaning herself vigorously and will then wish to compose herself for a fairly exhausted sleep. At this moment she should be cleaned up with cotton wool and warm water, to which a little T.C.P. has been added, and dried with clean cotton wool, given a clean bed and left alone, in the dark, for an hour or two to recover from her efforts. She may very thankfully accept a small bowl of warm milk to which a dessertspoonful of glucose has been added, or a Casilan drink, provided this is held for her and she has to make little effort over it.

As soon as the puppies arrive, the temperature of the room should be really warm, and our own puppies are kept at a temperature of seventy degrees for the first three days, steadily decreasing thereafter to normal temperature after a week. We would stress very forcibly that warmth is one of the essential factors in rearing a healthy litter, and it is something that is within scope of the human. The puppies will be fully occupied for the first three days in getting a strong hold on life and in dealing with the job of feeding, and if they are not kept very warm it may be just too much effort for the smallest or least lively in the litter. So make your arrangements well in advance to give the puppies plenty of regulated steady warmth to ensure they maintain their grip on life.

After the puppies are safely on their way in this world, and the mother has had a peaceful and uninterrupted sleep, you should lift her from her babies and take her to her usual place in the garden so that she may relieve herself. She must be allowed back immediately as she will be in a rather hypersensitive state and must not feel that she is being kept from her precious babies for one minute longer than is necessary. When she has her babies safely cuddled to her again, she may like another drink. She should always have her dish held near to her, as many bitches are so attentive to their young that they will not leave them even to eat and drink. She should have every chance to pass a motion within twenty-four hours of whelping, and if she does not eliminate naturally, she must be given a glycerine suppository. A child's size suppository is the right size and this should be gently inserted into the rectum; and after about three to five minutes the necessary motion will be passed. She should be kept very quiet for the first three or four days with no strangers or children to see her, and certainly no other dogs. She has had a busy and anxious time and now the new babies will take all her attention, and she has no thought for anyone else. It is now especially that her privacy should be guarded, and she should feel doubly secure from intruders of any kind. It is our responsibility to see to this, and she must feel that she can trust us.

WEANING THE PUPPIES. The time for weaning rather depends on the number of puppies in the litter and also how

THE FIRST POODLE LITTER

the mother is standing the strain. But usually supplementary feeding of the puppies need not start until they are at least a month old. To start them off, one small meal a day of Sherley's Lactol or the Casilan mixture, mentioned previously, is ideal, and two to three teaspoonsful per puppy is ample. This should be given at blood heat, and one of the best methods is to sit the puppy on a towel on your lap, have the feed in a cup in a pan of hot water to keep the temperature even, and then put the right amount of the liquid into a small shallow dish (we always use a small coffee saucer) and dip the puppy's nose into the liquid. They will blow bubbles to begin with, but it is surprising how quickly they will lap. Be careful to wash off the milk from their faces, after each feed, with damp cotton wool, for if this is neglected a sour milk smell occurs which is most insanitary. After the third day, the feeds can be increased to two a day, and after that the puppies should have arrived at the stage when they can stand up and feed from a shallow dish by themselves. A good tip here is to make a little wooden stand about 1½in. high, on which the dish is placed. This will help the puppies to feed comfortably and will prevent them from overbalancing head first into the milk. At the end of a week of milky diet they can start on one small meal a day of scraped raw meat. This should be rolled into a little ball about the size of a marble, and if too "tacky" for them to eat, a little warm water can be added.

It is sometimes difficult to know exactly when the puppies should be started off on weaning food, but a fairly safe guide, which should warn us that the puppies are ready to wean, is when the dam starts regurgitating her food, or alternatively if the puppies begin to gather round the dam's dish. If the bitch vomits her food for the puppies, this is quite natural, and they should be allowed to consume this pre-digested food. But as soon as this takes place, the bitch should be fed with meals that are suitable for the puppies, i.e. minced raw meat and brown bread, or else cooked white fish. Be sure to give her a second meal for herself when she has regurgitated her first dinner for her puppies.

The puppies should be wormed at six weeks old, and again one of the safest vermifuges is Burroughs Wellcome's "Banocide"—probably a quarter of a tablet for a Miniature Poodle puppy, and if this is given in a little thick honey, the puppy will not vomit after the dose.

Be careful that the rectums of the puppies do not become soiled or blocked, and a daily inspection is recommended as the dam does not always attend to this regularly. If the skin is at all pink or sore, a little zinc and castor oil ointment will put this right.

Between the ages of four and eight days, the tails will have to be docked and the dew claws, both back and front, removed. For your guidance about half the tail should be removed, or the width of a shilling left on.

The dam will need no regular exercise for at least a month, in fact it is far better that she does not go on to the highway or to any place where she might pick up infection while the puppies are very young. You should be careful to nip off the needle-sharp points of the nails on the front feet of the puppies when they are about ten days old and again every week after that. These sharp little needle points can really cause a bitch agony and make her very sore indeed, and she may well be reluctant to feed them or become very bad tempered if you neglect this very important job. Also it is essential that the bitch should have some place in her kennel or room where she can get away from her babies at various times in the day; the best thing is a rug or sack on top of her box where she can jump and where the puppies cannot follow. She will much appreciate this.

Your little Poodle bitch has done all you asked of her and she has provided you with a quality litter of valuable puppies; and for this you have an obligation towards her. She deserves the best you can do for her in return. She must not have her babies ruthlessly taken away from her *en masse* at six weeks old, and they must be removed one by one. Perhaps the better method is to take her away for increasingly long periods at a time, during which she has special interests such as bones, walks and human companionship. She must be allowed to return to her babies every so often to satisfy herself that they are quite safe and well. She will gradually relinquish her hold on them. She must *never* be taken away from her puppies and shut up with other dogs in a kennel, as the mental anxiety and anguish to the bitch would be very great. Give her plenty of new interests at this time with added home comforts and she will then quickly forget the puppies which must of necessity go out into the world and start their own individual lives.

10

THE SMALL KENNEL OF POODLES

Kennels—Runs—Hygiene—Feeding—Vitamins.

You have now bred your first litter of Poodles, and since they looked a very nice healthy bunch of youngsters, and as you had used a really good stud dog, you feel you could not do better than keep two of the bitches to act as the nucleus for your small kennel. Hitherto you have probably had your Poodles in the house, but now that the numbers are beginning to mount you must consider the matter of outside kennels.

First and foremost, go to a good firm where the construction of kennels is thoroughly understood. Do not invest in flimsy kennels, nor the home-made type, because they will not stand up to hard wear. Give your Poodles plenty of room, remembering that this kennel is your Poodle's home for a good part of the day. Strong, sturdy timber with well-fitting doors will reduce draught to a minimum. If you can afford a corridor kennel you will never regret it, as it makes feeding and cleaning out so much easier in bad weather, and also affords the dogs a greater degree of company and light than in the ordinary single kennel. See that your kennels either face the rising sun or the setting sun, preferably the former, although you also in this case get the full force of the east wind. Kennels facing south are lovely in spring, autumn and winter, but very hot in the summer, while those facing west catch the prevailing rain quite frequently. If your kennels are well and strongly constructed, and if possible lined with plywood or boarding, then your dogs will need no heating in winter providing they are given deep beds filled with clean straw to a depth of at least 18in. The straw should be changed every week and topped up mid-week. If the floors of your kennels are covered with linoleum you will find it an easy matter to wash over these every morning with warm water and Dettol or Milton, or one of the cheaper disinfectants, and this will keep the kennels sweet smelling and healthy and free from any unpleasant odours.

You will need to give some thought to types of runs, and I would advise if possible a variety of these. Certainly the run outside your kennel or kennels should be concrete for easy cleaning in bad weather. Equally a grass run should be available for more vigorous exercise and also so that the Poodles may graze fresh grass when they need it, as grass is an essential medicinal property for all dogs. A loose gravel run is good for feet, but difficult to keep clean and also the small stones are dangerous when puppies are around.

A really essential part of kennel management is that all droppings must be picked up once a day, for at least two reasons. One, because flies will collect on neglected droppings and then settle on food and contaminate it; and secondly, daily examination of fæces does give you a good picture of the health of your dogs. Any tendency to constipation or diarrhoea can be seen at once, and also the presence of worms. Newspaper is probably the best floor covering for young puppies, and this should be changed two or three times a day and immediately burnt. Sawdust is an alternative but this does get into Poodles' coats and eyes, and is also difficult to burn or get rid of. An incinerator is essential, and daily burning must be carried out. The usual galvanized type with a wire bottom and lid is very satisfactory, and we would suggest one with galvanized sides rather than wire sides, because in the latter the straw is apt to blow about everywhere in a high wind. Fresh water must always be available, and if your Poodles have the irritating habit of overturning water bowls just for the fun of seeing the water flow, then the smallest size of galvanized bucket hung on a hook about 6in. from the ground is a good idea and stops "Poodle paddling". If you have any male Poodles you may care to erect a post about 4ft. high and 1ft. in the ground, and cover this round with straw and bind with string or wire. You will find the dogs will use this for relieving themselves and it does reduce the fouling of the sides of kennels, gate posts, etc. The straw can then be changed weekly to keep it hygienic.

Poodles need as much exercise as you can give them, and while the house dog gets most of his exercise by running about the house and garden each day, the kennel dogs *must* have daily walks to keep them in hard and healthy condition. Good hard road walking at a brisk pace is excellent for muscling up feet

PLATE V. A brother and sister in serviceable lamb trim.
Photo: Margaret Worth

PLATE VI. "Rothara Wychwood the Spark", the 9½" winning Toy Poodle belonging to Mrs. Sheldon and Miss Lockwood. *Photo: Fall*

PLATE VII (*above*) "Are yo as nosey as I am?" "Lulu working with two of Fran and Margaret Worth glove puppets.
Photo: Margaret Wor

PLATE VIII (*left*) A Miniatur Poodle demonstrating he training in heel work for th Obedience Ring.
Photo: Margaret Wor

Lamb cut

Colour photos by Anne Cumbers

Toy Poodle's first puppy cut at 6 weeks old

Snowstar Silver Miniature Poodles with puppy cut

Toy Poodle Snowstar Miguel: owner Mrs Gregory

Judging Miniature Poodles

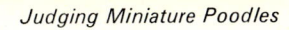

Toy Poodle with lion cut: ch. Snowstar Sarachi

Toy Poodle bitch with puppies at 1 week old

Snowstar Toy Poodle puppies at 4 weeks old

and quarters. Narrow round leather collars are most suitable for Poodles, as flat leather or chain choke collars rub off the coat round the neck.

The feeding of your Poodles should be a matter of major consideration, but provided you bear in mind that the three essentials are quality, variety and balance, then your Poodles should do well. First, good quality food is absolutely essential and well worth the little extra cost. You cannot expect a stud dog or a brood bitch to produce well if fed on lights, paunch and other offal. For condition they must have good red meat, fed raw if possible. If your Poodles do not like raw meat, then either roast the meat for them or stew it until just cooked. If you stew the meat, the liquor in which it is cooked must be used too, as this will contain so much of the goodness from the meat. Variety is essential, and you will find Poodles will eat much better if they do not have the same food placed in front of them every day. Ring the changes by giving them raw meat, then roast or stewed, sometimes with soaked biscuit, sometimes with dry biscuit. And lastly see that your Poodles have balance in their diet—there must be a large amount of protein (meat, eggs, fish, etc.) and there must be a proportion of carbohydrates (biscuit and cereal) in the daily diet, and a small amount of fat either on the meat or given in the form of a teaspoonful of shredded suet over the food each day.

If you can get butcher's meat this will be well worth the added expense. Knacker's meat is readily obtainable for dogs, but in these days when drugs are so widely used for farm animals, it is always a risk. It may be safe for months, and then you might be unlucky and start up a long and worrying poisoning amongst your dogs. It is possible to get both ox cheeks and frozen skirts at a fairly reasonable price and sometimes even frozen hind-quarter from the butcher. But for puppy feeding it is well worth buying frozen shin or some other moderately lean cut of beef, but you must ensure that this is well thawed out before feeding to either adult dogs or puppies.

Poodles should have a good drink of milk after their daily exercise, and those who have a busy stud programme, or heavy showing fixtures, and pregnant and nursing bitches, should have plenty of raw eggs either beaten up in milk, or broken over the meat.

Provided quality, variety and balance are borne in mind, very few extra vitamins are necessary. Vitamin D is perhaps the best vitamin of the lot, being contained in sunshine. In the winter to take the place of sunshine, a daily dose of cod liver oil may be given (two teaspoonsful for large Poodles, one teaspoonful for miniatures and a half-teaspoonful for toys), or else four, two or one drop of halibut liver oil respectively. These fish oils are strong in Vitamins A and D, and are excellent disease resisters and also assist in the steady and healthy growth of youngsters. Vitamin E, which is particularly necessary for fertility, is to be found in Wheat Germ oil. A ten day course of Wheat Germ oil is of great value two or three times a year for both stud dogs and brood bitches. Raw parsley and grated raw carrot are valuable additions to a dog's diet, being very strong in Vitamin A. The condition of the skin is kept healthy by the administration of Vitamin B.1., while the nervous system is toned up with Vitamin B.2., both of these being found in yeast, liver, wheat germ, milk, meat and eggs. Dogs are known to produce their own Vitamin C, so it is not an important point, but again this vitamin is contained in milk, and strongly in grass. But provided your Poodle has plenty of meat, milk, and eggs, with a small amount of a good quality biscuit as roughage, he should grow into a healthy specimen of the breed.

We hope that this booklet will in some small measure have assisted our readers to rear their Poodle safely and easily, bringing him to trouble-free and happy maturity, when it will be found that he is the most lovable, most companionable and most intelligent breed that it is possible to own.

11

DOG SHOWS AND SHOW PROCEDURE

There are five types of Dog Shows, all of which are held under the Kennel Club's rules and regulations; they are as follows:

1. Exemption Shows. These are very small shows usually held in conjunction with fetes and flower shows during the summer months. There are usually four classes for pedigree dogs of all varieties, and any number of comic classes such as the Dog with the Longest Tail, the Largest Eyes, etc., etc. Entries, usually one shilling or two shillings per class, are made at the show. These little shows are great fun and excellent training grounds for puppies.

2. Sanction Shows. These are small but more serious shows, where there may be as many as twenty classes, and you may be lucky and get a class for Poodles only. Only dogs who have not yet won a Challenge Certificate may attend these shows, and the highest class is Post Graduate, i.e. for dogs which have not won more than four first prizes, each of the value of £1 or more, in Post Graduate, Minor Limit, Mid. Limit, Limit, or Open Classes. The dogs are not "benched" and sit with their owners round the hall. Prize money is usually 10/- for first, 5/- for second, and 2/6d. for third, and the entry fee is about 3/- per class.

3. Limited Shows. These are usually for members only, and are also limited to dogs who have not won a Challenge Certificate, but are of a higher grade than Sanction Shows. The prize money is slightly higher, and entries usually cost 5/- per class. Limited Shows are often "benched", when there is a small extra charge or benching fee per dog. Breeds are usually divided and may have two or more classes each.

4. Open Shows. As the name implies these are open to all, without any restrictions. Prize money is £1, 10/-, and

5/-. Entry fee varies, the shows are usually "benched". Breeds have several classes each, and sometimes the sexes in the breeds are divided.

5. CHAMPIONSHIP SHOWS. These are the top shows of the Country with entries running into thousands. Challenge Certificates are provided in each breed (unless stated to the contrary in the schedule). Each breed has its own judge, and dogs and bitches are judged separately in most classes. Prize money is £2, £1 and 10/-. Entry fees are usually 12/6d. per class, with an additional 3/- per dog benching fee.

Challenge Certificates are awarded to the best dog and the best bitch in each breed, *providing* they are, in the judge's opinion up to the standard of quality to be a champion. A dog has to gain three such Certificates under three different judges in order to become a Champion. In all miniature breeds, should the dog gain three Certificates *before* the age of twelve months, it must under Kennel Club rules gain a further one *after* this age, before being granted the title of Champion. In some other countries, notably the U.S.A., dogs are made champions after gaining a certain number and quality of wins, and Champions are only shown against Champions. In this country, however, Champions continue to be shown in the Open Classes, and in order to gain a Challenge Certificate, one has to beat all other dogs, including Champions—a hard task indeed, but this method undoubtedly keeps the quality of our Champions very high. The Kennel Club has recently given a most stern directive to all judges, that in the event of the dogs brought before them failing to reach this standard, the Certificate is to be withheld.

Classes. There are many different classes; some are governed by age, such as *Special Puppy*, over six and under nine months; *Puppy*, over six and under twelve months; *Junior*, over six months and not over eighteen months; *Yearling*, over one year but under two years, etc. Others are governed by the number of previous wins the dog has had, such as *Special Beginners*, owner, handler, and dog, never having won a first prize. *Maiden:* Dog never having won a first prize. *Novice:* Not won more than two first prizes. *Debutant:* Never won a first prize at a Championship show, etc., etc.

DOG SHOWS AND PROCEDURE 67

Best in Show. At the end of the show or at a stated time during the show after all Breed classes have been judged, the Stewards will call for all unbeaten dogs and bitches. Thus all Best of Breed winners, provided they have not been beaten in a variety class, will enter the ring, as well as any winning unbeaten dog or bitch from the unclassified class, which is a variety class for all breeds of dogs which have no breed classes of their own. From this collection of unbeaten dogs the judge will then choose two; these may either be one of each sex, in which case the award is for Best in Show, and Best Opposite Sex, or two of the same sex, Best in Show and Reserve Best in Show. This, of course, is decided by the rules governing the Society running the show. At small, or at Breed shows, there is often an award for Best Puppy in show, so if you are showing a puppy and it is unbeaten in its class, be ready to compete for this.

How to Enter for a Show. The dates of forthcoming shows are published in the weekly Dog papers, *Our Dogs* and *The Dog World*, either of which can be obtained through your local newsagent. When you have decided which show you wish to attend, you should write to the Hon. Secretary for a schedule. When this arrives, study it very carefully, reading all the regulations and definitions of the classes. Enter your dog in the class suitable for its age, and it is wise not to enter in more than two classes at your first show. Fill in the entry form carefully, giving your dog's full registered name, and send this form, with the necessary cash, to the address given. The date that entries close is printed on the front of the Schedule, and no entries are accepted after this date.

Show Equipment. The equipment you will require to take with you depends very much on the type of show, and also on the quality of your dog. If it is a small unbenched afternoon show, and your dog's coat is not very profuse, you will only need your brush and comb, a few tit bits, and his ordinary collar and lead. But if it is a large benched show, lasting most of the day, your requirements will be considerably larger. Here is a list of equipment which is all useful, and the essentials are marked thus *:—

1. Small light folding table.
* 2. Small case or bag for your grooming kit, etc.
* 3. Bench rug of useful size. You can make a very nice one from an old blanket dyed to whatever colour shows off your dog best. If the blanket is thin, make it of double thickness, and bind it round with coloured carpet binding. This looks smart and gay, and does not wrinkle up on the bench. You may add an initial on the front, but not a name.
* 4. Bench chain. It is best to make this up yourself, as the ready-made ones are too long for Poodles. 18in. of light lavatory or lamp chain from any ironmonger, plus one large swivel clip at one end, and a smaller one at the other. These can be fixed to the chain by two split rings, and the large hook is attached to the ring at the back of the bench, the smaller, to your dog's collar.
* 5. Grooming kit, i.e. brush and comb.
6. Hair ribbon and rubber bands for top-knots.
* 7. Very small bottle of well diluted T.C.P. or Milton for internal use, and the same of strong disinfectant for external use. These are for disinfecting your dog at the end of the show, down his throat and over his feet, and are most essential.
8. Small tin containing tit bits.
9. For white Poodles small tin containing a little starch powder for cleaning off any dirt on anklets and paws collected on your way to the show. Poodles are not allowed under Kennel Club Rules to appear in the ring with powder in their coats.
*10. A small drinking dish and a bottle of milk or water for your dog.
*11. The schedule of the show and your exhibitor's pass.
*12. Safety-pin or clip for ring number card.

So much for your Poodle's requirements; now for your own: Dog shows are very tiring affairs, and as most of your time, when not in the judging ring is spent by your bench, a small folding stool, or lightweight folding chair, will add greatly to your comfort. Also the clothes you wear can make or mar your day, so the following hints may be useful.

DOG SHOWS AND PROCEDURE

1. If you intend to wear a hat, be sure your Poodle is used to this. Believe it or not, a young puppy can be completely thrown out of balance by his owner suddenly donning a never-before-seen affair on her head!
2. Do not wear a long loose coat, or a very wide skirt that will flap across your Poodle as he walks, as this will upset the dog and also obscure the judge's view.
3. Be sure your shoes are really comfortable, high heels on rough ground can be disastrous.
4. Bearing in mind the English weather, a very light plastic mackintosh should undoubtedly form part of your outfit.

Now as to food: Your dog will be better without food until after his classes are over, but you yourself cannot keep to this rule with success. The nervous strain of a dog show, even if you are an old hand, must be kept at bay with nourishing food. Often one does not feel like much breakfast before an early start, therefore a thermos of coffee for a hot drink on the way to the show, or at the show, as soon as your dog is comfortably settled, is a godsend.

Most of us have little time for making elaborate sandwiches before starting, but it is now possible to buy tubes of butter, cream cheese, tomato puree, etc., and these, with a few slices of bread, biscuits or scones, make a delightful fresh lunch. These tubes keep fresh for months, and are better not put in a refrigerator. Personally I always find a thermos of soup an excellent thing for winter shows, as it is warming, very nourishing, and has the advantage of taking no time at all to eat, a good point at a crowded show. A good idea for summer shows is any meat, fish or poultry left overs, mixed with a little tomato or any cold cooked vegetables, and put in a small plastic container, with a little salad cream to moisten—don't forget a spoon! A small bottle of diluted orange squash with added glucose, is very helpful, and in winter a dash of rum or whisky is pleasant!

At small afternoon shows a good tea buffet is usually available, and there is no need to take food with you.

On arrival at the show venue, you will be required to present your dog for examination by the attendant Veterinary

Surgeon. After this, you can proceed to your bench, the number of which is on your exhibitor's pass which will have been sent you by the show secretary. This entitles you and your dog to free entry.

As soon as you have settled your Poodle on his bench, get out your schedule and the catalogue which you have bought at the show entrance, and check your classes. If there should be any differences between the two, go straight to the show secretary's office and ask to see your entry form, which by Kennel Club rules has to be held in the office during the show. From this you can discover who is at fault, the catalogue or yourself. If the former, you are entitled to enter your correct class, but must inform the ring steward when you do so. If the fault is yours, then nothing can be done and you must miss your class and forfeit your money, so be sure to check those entries before posting them.

Having ascertained that your entries are in order, get your dog thoroughly brushed and combed. If his anklets or feet have got dirty, rub a little powder on them, and then brush it out. Wipe his nails with a damp sponge, tie up his top-knot, and then put him back on his bench until it is time to give him his final touches before entering the ring. It is as well to find out in advance exactly where your ring is situated. If you have trained your dog well at home he, or she, will be quite used to being tied up, and will rest quietly on the bench. It is your duty to train your dog in this way, so that he is not a nuisance to other exhibits. Noisy and fretting dogs are nothing to be proud of, and it is rare indeed to see one belonging to an experienced and efficient exhibitor. Also it is an extremely bad advertisement for Poodles as a breed; the public does not admire the excitable, unhappy exhibit, whose owner has taken no trouble to train him before the show, or to make him feel happy and comfortable on his bench.

If you have a little spare time before your first class, this is the time to have that cup of coffee or soup; remember you have a long day in front of you, and you will show your dog better if you take care of yourself in this way.

When the time approaches for your class, give your dog his final brush up; memorize your number from the card above your bench; also just check up on his age; then *carry* him into the ring. I think this is most important, as a stepped-on paw in the crowd, or a growl from another dog, may well upset him and spoil his chances. On entering the ring go straight to the steward and ask for your ring card, stating your dog's number, not his name (this card must be affixed to your person where it is clearly visible), then take up your position with the other new dogs. Dogs which have appeared in a previous class are placed on a different side of the ring from the new dogs.

When you are handling an inexperienced dog, it is as well to stand at the bottom of the line in order to give him time to settle down. This "bottom of the line" is a coveted place in the early classes, and it is an amusing sight to see the old hands jockeying for this position with polite "after you's" to each other! You will probably have a few minutes before the judging starts to make much of your dog, and to make him forget any show nerves; your own you must stifle; many experienced handlers still suffer from this after years of showing. One good thing to remember is that the judge and the ring-siders are not interested in *you* but your dog, so try to forget yourself and concentrate on your job in hand.

If you have followed the advice in this book, you will have already attended a show or two as a spectator, and will know the routine, and will have practised this at home, with your Poodle. Remember to let your dog relax while other exhibits are being examined, but have him set up looking his best by the time the judge has finished with his last entry.

There is only one thing more you need possess, and that is self-control and sense of proportion. Remember there are only *four* award cards in every class, no matter how many dogs are entered, or how good they are; therefore it is often no disgrace not to be placed. Also, no two judges think alike, it would indeed be dull if they did so; but it is very hard indeed not to show one's disappointment when not placed, especially if one considers, as one usually does, that the dog involved is not as good as one's own! However, there is always another day, another show, and a different judge.

After your dog has finished his classes it is as well to pour a little of the diluted disinfectant down his throat, and to wipe his paws with your disinfected sponge. I always do this again on leaving the show.

Unless you have applied for an "Early Removal", you must remain at the show until closing time, and remember, it is a

Kennel Club rule that at a benched show no dog may be absent from its bench for more than fifteen minutes, except when actually in the ring. This rule is made in order that the public who have paid for entry may be able to see the dogs. The breaking of this rule can bring disqualification of any prize won.

At an unbenched show, this of course, does not apply, and you and your dog can sit where you like, providing he is not on the floor of the ring.

12

SOME POODLE TALES

The "Boss" of the Kennels—Alarm on the Eve of Crufts—Adventures on the High Seas.

WE suppose in every kennel, one dog is the "boss"; and in this kennel "Rothara the Rake" is certainly the acknowledged leader. He is a benign and elegant dog, but it is quite obvious that all the Poodles, male and female, respect him, and his word is law. He is infinitely intelligent, long suffering with youngsters, and seems to have that quality of knowing exactly what is said to him and is always out to do his best with the least fuss. He has also been trained as a guard dog, for we live in the country and value his protection. He has a deep and forbidding bark and would not allow any intruder into the house. He is invaluable for seeing off the various tramps and pedlars who wander into our drive from the main road.

The "Rake's" triumphs in the show ring have been many, for he has no less than ninety First prizes to his credit and has been judged Best in Show All Breeds, fourteen times. His name appears in most white Miniature Poodle pedigrees to-day, and he has progeny in Australia, France, New Zealand, Canada, Switzerland, and, of course, the United States.

His leadership of the kennels was only once challenged, and then by his son US/CH. Rothara the Cavalier. Words were exchanged and both suffered slight damage, more to their dignity than to their bodies, and ever after they would stand back to back grumbling loudly at each other, but it never went further than that after the first scuffle—and "Rake" remained supreme. His life has not been without incident, for to begin with he was born "dead". He was one of a litter of three dogs, and while the first two were born very easily to his mother, Rothara Honey Dew, the third proved difficult. After a certain amount of trouble (and great skill on the part of our lady Veterinary Surgeon, Mrs. Green), a miserable looking object, greenish in colour and quite flat, with a distinctly blue face, was eventually produced. This obviously dead puppy was put with the rubbish while the vet. was attending to the mother. However, the vet. said there was just a hope of reviving this puppy and she thereupon set to work with warm towels, artificial respiration, and massage of the heart, but all to no avail. We were on the point of giving up all our efforts when to our joy and surprise the puppy gave a very faint gasp, then a gulp, and it was obvious that his lungs had begun to function. Efforts were redoubled and within ten minutes the puppy was transformed into a moderately rounded, normal coloured youngster eagerly nuzzling his mother for his first meal—and that was "Rothara the Rake".

He had yet another unpleasant experience when about eighteen months old. We were spending the night in London prior to attending Crufts Show on the following day, and had the "Rake" with us as our only entry that year. On our arrival in London "Rake" was duly taken into Hyde Park in the late afternoon for a run, and we then returned to our hotel. Just before going to bed, we noticed that his face looked strange, and even as we watched him we realized that his head, ears, face and paws were visibly swelling every minute. We tried frantically to locate a vet., but the first one was away for the week-end, the second was in bed with 'flu; but the third time we were lucky and got in touch with a lady vet. in Kensington. She told us not to worry, but to get him to her by taxi immediately. This, of course, we did with the utmost speed. By this time "Rake's" head and face resembled a boxer's more than a Poodle's and we were quite certain he was going to die. The vet. gave him an immediate injection and told us he was suffering from some sort of allergy, and that she had had no less than seventeen Crufts entries brought in to her that evening with the same symptoms, and "Rake" was lucky enough to have the last injection she had in stock. She told us that we could expect the swelling to subside and that he would suffer no ill-effects. This all happened at the time of the death of King George VI, and many salvos had been fired in Hyde Park. It was thought that some dogs were allergic to the powder used for this purpose, since so many who had been in the Park that day were showing the same symptoms. We took our much loved Poodle back to our hotel, and on the way up the few stairs to our rooms, he stumbled and then collapsed, and we carried an unconscious dog to his bed. Imagine our anxiety; we sat beside him and watched and waited. Certainly the swelling was abating, and his face and paws were becoming normal, but he was still unconscious. Suddenly, to our surprise, about four a.m. he opened his eyes, got up, shook himself, went over to his dish which contained his dinner. This he quickly ate with relish, drank his fill of water and then settled himself in his bed to sleep for another four hours. He woke at eight a.m., appeared quite normal, and we took him to Crufts where he showed to perfection and was placed second in a large class!

One of his greatest triumphs was the winning of the Best in Show award at a large show in Bristol. It was Whit-Monday and the crowds were dense; the day was swelteringly hot and there were over forty Bests of Breed in the large ring awaiting the decision of the three judges. "Rake" gave everything he had, and stood for no less than fifty minutes, never moving a muscle, but just quivering the tip of his tail. The judges were minutely examining each dog and gradually the process of elimination began. First there were twenty dogs left in the ring, then fifteen, then ten, and so it went on until there were only two; and then the decision was unanimously given and "Rake" had won Best in Show out of something like a thousand dogs! He seemed to know that the suspense was over for he went round the ring like a king, barking joyously to the loud and long applause from the spectators. He then lay in his bench nonchalantly accepting the congratulations and praise of the many hundreds who came to look at him, and who came to admire the array of silver cups laid out on the table in front of his bench. His showing days are now over and his thoughts are more upon matrimonial matters, but he ended his show career by gaining Best in Show at three successive shows within the space of a fortnight, and adding no less than eleven silver challenge cups to his collection.

Our first Poodle, grandmother of "The Rake" was also a most dominant character, and always managed to achieve exactly what she wanted. She had a wicked habit of being able to open almost any latch. We had put a slam catch on the gate of the paddock thinking this would defeat "Roxie". But no, she could press the knob and open the gate easily. So we transferred the catch to the outside of the gate and fixed a piece of string so that by pulling this we could open the gate from the inside. But "Roxie" also quickly worked out the mechanics of this, for she used to take the string in her teeth and pull, at the same time pushing the gate with her front feet; and then the gate would swing open. But her guile did not end there. At the opening of the gate the other dogs would rush through and into the house, where they would be soundly reprimanded, while "Roxie" herself would smugly stay in the paddock, and no doubt if she could have spoken she would have said, "Look at those Poodles, aren't they naughty?" It is interesting to note that "Rake", her grandson, is now doing exactly the same trick, and while a slam catch foils all the other poodles, "Rake" opens them with the greatest of ease and has the same habit of letting the others surge through and take the blame, while he stays in the run and watches the result.

There is no doubt that Poodles have the capacity for twisting humans round their little paws, and revelling in it. "Roxie" had arrived at the age when she was due for all the home comforts possible, a place by the fire in winter, freedom from the irritating pranks of young and boisterous Poodles, and a quiet life away from the hurry and flurry of kennels. Some friends of ours had always wanted her to go to live with them in her late middle age, and so at last she moved into her new home. Up till then she had been used to a good bed of straw in a dog house accommodating seven other Poodles, and she had always lived with "The Rake", having the usual kennel diet of raw meat, milk, biscuits, etc. After she had been in her new home a few weeks, our friends rang up to say that "Roxie" had settled wonderfully and was a great joy to them, but she was a little difficult over her food as she refused to eat anything but boiled chicken and the top off the milk, and that she always insisted on a saucer of milk to which had been added a teaspoonful of whisky on going to bed, and only remained quiet at night if she was covered all over with a light rug and slept in a basket by her owner's bed. It just proves that if you give Poodles an inch they will take an ell, and before you can turn round they will be ruling you with a rod of iron!

"The Rake" was responsible for an interesting rescue story: His grandson, Rothara the Riot, with whom he had been kennelled for some months, was going to a new home, but on the way there his new owners stopped their car in the New Forest and as they opened the car door "Riot" slipped out. Of course, he did not really know his new owners and took fright and was away into the forest. A long and exhausting search was made, lasting three days and nights, and although a white Poodle was seen many times in the distance he could never be caught. We went to the aid of his new owners and tramped many miles calling and shouting his name, and the names of all his kennel mates in the hope that he might come to us, but there was no sign, although his tracks were clearly seen in the mud, and tufts of white hair were noticed on the brambles. At last it was suggested that he might come out if he saw "The Rake", his kennel mate; so "Rake" was walked for miles in the Forest, but still no sign of "Riot". But the next morning it was noticed that wherever "Rakes" footprints were, there also were the marks of the smaller feet of "Riot". The time of year was the end of January, but luckily it was mild and there was no snow or frost, and thus tracks were easily seen in the soft mud. To everyone's great joy after three and a half days of fruitless search and anxiety, a bedraggled, tired and very hungry little white Poodle came hesitantly out of the undergrowth and joined up with his grandfather "Rothara the Rake". So the experiment had worked, and within three weeks the wanderer was again in the show ring, and since then has been the constant companion of his devoted owner, and has many First prizes and Bests in Show to his credit. A happy ending to a dreadful three and a half days.

An amusing incident occurred once when we were caravanning and also taking our dogs to Leeds Championship Show. We had selected a very pretty little glade in which to park our caravan where there was plenty of short turf for exercising the Poodles. The dogs always slept in "Goddard" beds in the back of our shooting brake, and had specially made long and voluminous Teddy Bear cloth dressing-gowns to keep them warm during the night. They were duly tucked up for the night, and we retired to the caravan by the side of the car. During the night there was considerable and unceasing rain, and to our horror when we looked out in the morning we found our glade was a lake and we were completely marooned, surrounded by more than a foot of water. About twenty yards away there was a small grass mound with a bush on it. So we donned our gum boots, and each shining spotless white Poodle in immaculate show trim was carefully carried through the water to the small mound, where each one solemnly performed his or her duty, and was carefully carried back and all was well. A case of complete co-operation between owner and exhibit!

Some years ago we sent a white Poodle and a black Poodle to New Zealand, both of which are now New Zealand Champions. These dogs had two large kennels on the top deck, and before leaving had been introduced to the ship's butcher, which was a strategic move, and this young man was obviously very fond of dogs. All went well during the voyage but apparently it was the hottest trip they had yet experienced. The dogs were exercised on leads on the deck by the butcher, and believe it or not the black Poodle, "Rothara the Blacksmith", managed to roll in some white paint, while the white dog "Rothara the Scallywag" had his coat covered with black tar which was melting on the deck in the extreme heat. In an effort to help, the dogs were then washed down on the hottest days with the hose! The result was disastrous, and two curious looking Poodles greeted their new owners in Wellington. However they were in wonderful physical condition, and although their coats had to be cut short, they quickly grew, and within a few months they had both gained their New Zealand Championships.

We exported a dear little white Poodle bitch to Australia many years ago, and as the purchaser wished her to be mated before she left England, the time element needed a great deal of careful planning. However, luck was on our side as she came in season and was mated just the day before the boat was due to leave. There was only one possible sailing each month and the voyage takes nearly six weeks. In view of the fact that a surcharge of £5 is made on each puppy born aboard ship, it was desirable that she did not have her family until after she arrived in Australia. This she did, and walked out of quarantine with five lovely white puppies sired by "Rothara the Rake". She was the only Poodle in that particular ship, and as the First Officer was a great dog lover she became his constant companion. We gather she spent little time in her deck kennel and her usual place was on the officer's bunk.

The boat was due to arrive in Australia on Christmas Day, and so our little white bitch was the guest of honour at the ship's Christmas party, and attended this function in a paper hat and a ruffle, and waddled round heavily in whelp. Certainly all the puppies should have been good sailors!

We think that the following story of "Lulu" will interest our readers, for it tells of her life as a live artiste in a troupe of Glove Puppets which are one of the hobbies of Mr. and Mrs. Worth, and which have given such immense pleasure to so many children in England. Mrs. Worth writes:—

"Lulu"—eight weeks old and completely fascinating. She was our first Poodle and was to be a Toby in our Punch and Judy show. She obviously had brains and energy and soon developed a character and a flair for getting her own way. Her early puppyhood was a delight, full of unusually graceful and skilful play. But she had been bought for a purpose and so her training began.

We made her a ruffle, a broad scarlet silk frill. She wore it like a queen, never an attempt to get it off, but a complete acceptance of it. She sat at the playing ledge and became part of the show. The puppets fed her and talked to her and she watched their antics with interest, but her quick-silver quality was lost, and we felt that her role there was altogether too static, although our audiences were obviously delighted to see a "live" dog. We decided on a floor show with "Lulu" before the Puppet show opened.

Her first tricks came out of her natural aptitude for jumping. With a hoop held 3in. from the ground, and her lead passed through it, we gave her the command, "Over", pulled her through, and then gave her a tiny tit bit. That was sufficient; she was back through the hoop and quickly learnt to jump a surprising height with very little take off. The command "Over", meant jump, and in no time at all she would jump over my raised leg, my outstretched arm, or through the circle formed by my arms when my hands were joined. Having got so far we tried her on an audience, and our education began, as well as "Lulu's". What had seemed quite a performance at home appeared to us much less impressive in public. But the response was surprising. Both adults and children were full of enthusiasm, and "please will you bring the wonderful little white Poodle", became a regular request with show bookings.

The children's pleasure in "Lulu" took the form of an urgent and often aggressive desire to fondle and pet her after the show. We had to protect her from this because, although friendly and confident, she was obviously overwhelmed by it. We made a light wooden travelling box in the form of a little house, with a door and windows. One half of the red roof formed a lid, and "Lulu" was soon hopping in and out with her usual agility. This house satisfied everyone. We knew that she was settled while the puppet show was on, "Lulu" knew that she was safe, and the children loved her house and were content to see her and talk to her through the windows. After this, parties held no terrors for "Lulu", and she faced Bank Holiday crowds with the aplomb of a seasoned star.

One thing that we had not bargained for was "Lulu's" "temperament". She is an enthusiastic artiste and thrives on adulation and applause; in fact, I have known her to walk out in front of the audience and take a bow, when the clapping at the end of the puppet show began, certain that any appreciation must be for her only. But she had other ideas too; she liked to do things in her own way and would start to jump the moment her hoops were produced and having done what she considered her quota, would refuse to do more unless under pressure. This determination to run her own show applied to each item as her repertoire increased. She quickly realized that she could get away with things at shows that we should not pass at home. She learned to dance. This consisted of pirouetting on her hind legs. We always insisted on at least three pirouettes before she dropped on all fours when rehearsing; and then she developed an annoying habit which cropped up again later in her more formal training. She would do all that was asked of her when rehearsing, so that no correction or training was needed, and then revert to her own ideas at shows when no correction could be given. For instance, she would pirouette once and then beg. There she would sit with her little front paws tucked up under her chin looking the picture of mischievous innocence. Nothing would move her, except the touch of my toe on one of her hind feet, whereupon she would perform one more pirouette, and again beg.

Our determination hardened, and we decided that the discipline of formal obedience training would help to solve

SOME POODLE TALES

our problems. Before we embarked on this new career, however, "Lulu" took on the responsibilities of motherhood. She managed this, as she did everything else, capably and independently. The week before her puppies were born, and on what happened to be her own first birthday, we were asked to bring her, with the show, to a little girl's birthday party. We explained the situation, but all that mattered to the child was that "Lulu" came with us. She came, complete with tiny cake and one candle, but again we had reckoned without our Poodle's personality. She was "on the job", and she knew it, and insisted on giving her usual performance.

Her four pups were born ten minutes after she came in from a walk. In fact she ran the last two hundred yards at full speed in order to reach home in time! They were born with a minimum of fuss and "Lulu" established a sensible routine straight away. No modern babies were more strictly brought up, or more rigorously disciplined. By the time that they were six weeks old, they were all following mother through the hoop!

"Lulu" is still learning new tricks and we are still learning too. We find that even with a quick eager dog, there are limitations, and that a mistake on our part may hold up training for some considerable time. We have never managed to persuade her to jump up into our arms, and yet her daughter did it at once. One day when we were teaching "Lulu" to weave in and out of our legs as we walked along, we inadvertently kicked her. It has taken months of patient encouragement to overcome this mishap and even now she is very wary.

13

POODLES AND OBEDIENCE TRAINING

WE have asked Mrs. Margaret Worth, the well known Obedience Trainer and Handler, to write the following chapter on this aspect of a Poodle's activities, and we are most indebted to her.

It is the opinion of a number of Poodle fanciers that the Obedience ring is not the place for this intelligent breed. The argument being that such a lively, sensitive dog quickly becomes bored with the routine and discipline of obedience work. Surely any breed will become bored with training that is dull and lifeless. The beauty ring offers much less variety of opportunity, but the dogs must look gay and lively to show well, and it is up to the handler to bring the best out of his dog. From my experience, the average pet Poodle suffers to a much greater degree through lack of mental and physical outlet than either the beauty ring or the obedience trained dog.

Being a member and trainer at an all breeds dog training club, and having trained both Collies and Poodles, I have come to the conclusion that the mental equipment of each individual dog is the thing that matters and not so much the breed, although some breeds have certain inherent qualities which make them easier to train for competition. Apart from this aspect of training, I think that every dog and dog owner benefits a great deal from a course of obedience within a club. The education by these very popular clubs is, of course, for the dog owners.

Certain basic principles of behaviour are essential in all dogs, and the novice handlers are shown the best methods of achieving these. Before you can embark on any competition training you must be able to control your dog quietly and efficiently and he must understand that you are to be obeyed. This is just as important for the pet as it is for the performer. Your dog must learn to walk quietly by your side both on and off the lead, he must learn to remain seated while you walk away from him, to bear himself with dignified self-control among others of his kind and, above all, he must learn to come when he is called. If, at the same time, you can teach him to retrieve an article to your hand, you will then own a dog that is a pride and a pleasure to take out, and the capacity to retrieve will give him the opportunity for a spell of hard exercise without going for a long walk. You cannot teach him these things at the club. During the weekly training hour you are the learner. You learn what to teach your dog, and how to teach it, and individual problems are dealt with as they arise. The dog's training must be done by you whenever you can spare the time. Twenty minutes every day, if possible, will achieve surprising results. It soon becomes apparent in a class, which dogs and handlers are doing their homework!

By the end of six months you will find that you have a sensibly behaved pet, and then, if you have any aptitude as a handler, you will want to try your luck in competition. Take warning. It is easy to step into the show ring, but not so easy to step out again. You will soon find yourself anxiously scanning the advertisements in one of the dog papers for shows within a reasonable distance of your home.

It was a Poodle, or perhaps I should say "the" Poodle, that led me into obedience competition. For "Lulu" is not just a trained dog, she has that touch of brilliance that lifts her above the epithet ordinary. She has only to catch a whisper of the word "Fun" and she is up, poised and ready, her eyes shining like stars. Now she had to learn the word "work", and to respond in the right way to commands, whether she wanted to obey or not, and without too much of her originality creeping in. Her eagerness needed harnessing without curbing.

"Lulu" has two great assets; she obviously enjoys learning and doing, and she has the power, so necessary in the obedience worker, of concentrated attention on her handler. In this pleasure in work she really does confound the critics and delight the spectators. She has taken part in many demonstrations and is invariably sought out afterwards and congratulated on such a happy performance.

The one piece of training equipment frequently criticised by Poodle lovers is the slip-chain. The slip-chain is a noose that hangs loosely round the dog's neck, but tightens when the lead is jerked, and loosens immediately the lead is slackened. It is a useful and effective form of correction and I have never known a dog resent it. "Lulu", however, has always been accustomed to the very lightest of whale-hide show leads and has done all her obedience training on this. Her heel-work has suffered nothing in accuracy, and so it seems to me that where you have a dog whose coat may suffer from the rub of the slip-chain, provided that the dog is alert and co-operative, the chain may be dispensed with.

In this chapter it is not my intention to give details of training from special beginners up to Test C; there are many books available now, devoted entirely to the subject. Rather, I wish to give a picture of a tiny miniature Poodle, whose temperament and intelligence so true to her breed, has proved her capable of enjoying work as well as play. And through this to encourage others to try their luck at this fascinating hobby. No dog is good at everything and one is apt to watch a trained dog's finished performance and imagine that it must have been easy to achieve. Nothing is farther from the truth. The usual recipe given to the novice handler is patience. I would add another ingredient and that is persistence. If you have a likely dog, never give in on one exercise that proves a stumbling block, but keep cheerfully trying, and do be lavish with praise and relaxation when your dog has done his best.

"Lulu" and I graduated from the training ground to the show ring one sunny Whit-Monday. We tied for first place in Test A. Encouraged by this success, we began to enter as many shows as possible, and to mix with the more experienced workers. This in itself is an asset, because a great deal can be learned by watching others, and a higher standard is aimed at. It was not long before "Lulu's" old habit reappeared: she would work perfectly in training and then produce an idea of her own in the show ring. First of all she got up in the two minute sit, almost as soon as I had left her, and followed me across the ring, and stood just behind me. Although she gave me no chance to correct this fault during training, I used such a firm tone in the ring that she decided to do something else. At the next show she quietly stood at every halt in the heel-work, instead of sitting! I countered this by going right back to basic training and used hand and lead at every halt. Our heel-work was faultless at our next competition, and I looked down into two affectionate liquid dark eyes, as she sat beside me, and wondered what little plot she was hatching this time. I soon found out. As I stepped away from her in the two minute sit, she did not follow me, but gently lay down and remained down for the rest of this exercise. "Lulu" repeated this at the following show, and so I subjected her to spells of sitting in the middle of the lawn, while I worked at the kitchen sink! What next, I wondered, and she did not disappoint me, but used her ingenuity on the retrieve. First she brought the dumbell back and stood before me, instead of sitting, and we lost a mark for an extra command. We had words on this subject and the next time she changed her tactics. She went out with her usual eagerness, raced up to the dumbell, looked at it, and came back without it. Once more that irritating extra command spoiled a perfect finish.

At this juncture I began to take stock of the whole situation, for although during this phase, we might be placed third or reserve, I felt that "Lulu" was unreliable. And then it struck me that she fell from grace in the exercises where I least expected it. I revised my own attitude at shows, and decided that I relaxed on exercises that I considered safe and this was my undoing. I expected "Lulu" to concentrate and I must do likewise. It was no use thinking that any exercise was foolproof, but the same care and firmness was needed for each one.

Having decided on a plan of campaign we set off, full of hope, on a bright August morning. The show was a popular one and "Lulu" was one in a class of seventeen dogs, fourteen of which were Alsatians. By this time I was familiar with show routine, and had begun to enjoy the ring-side gossip of other enthusiasts. With "Lulu" safely benched, I talked dogs to another early arrival. He was responsible for two of the fourteen Alsatians. During the course of conversation, his attention was caught by the lively barking from the toy Poodle benches. "Look at the poor little things", he said scathingly, "bred down to the size of rats." I looked, but naturally made no comment. At last my turn came, I fetched "Lulu". My new-found friend looked at her "Great Scott!" he said in apologetic amazement, "and I thought you were in Alsatians". "No, only rats!" I replied with a grin, as I entered the ring. The outcome of course is obvious, "Lulu" received her first coveted red card, and the sincere congratulations of the owner of the two Alsatians.

Obedience work was originally the province of Alsatians only; now it is open to all breeds, including cross-breeds, anyone who owns a dog may partake of its joys and sorrows. The beauty fancy has not been slow to seize this new opportunity for their dogs, and already there are several dual champions. The Poodle, whose sporting forebears make him peculiarly apt at learning, is to be seen more and more frequently in the Obedience ring. One Miniature has achieved the status of Obedience Champion. Surely it will not be long before this unique breed proves to the world that it has intelligence second to none, as well as grace, elegance and beauty.

Certainly once we have owned a Poodle we shall never regret it nor readily turn to any other breed. So often do people say "Oh, I don't want a Poodle, I want a dog that *is* a dog but my wife (or my daughter, or my friend) has set her heart on a Poodle". And then a few weeks later one learns that he who wanted a dog that *was* a dog, is now devoted to the Poodle, and is more than ready to agree with you that for intelligence and unfailing sense of humour, complete companionship and sheer beauty, there is no breed that even approaches our friend—the Poodle.

APPENDIX I

KENNEL CLUB STANDARD OF THE BREED

January 1950 (Reprinted October 1951)
Reproduced by kind permission of the Kennel Club,
1-4, Clarges Street, Piccadilly, London, W.1.

POODLE

GENERAL APPEARANCE. That of a very active, intelligent, and elegant-looking dog, well built, and carrying himself very proudly.

HEAD AND SKULL. Head long and straight and fine, the skull not broad, with a slight peak at the back. Muzzle long (but not snipy) and strong—not full in cheek, lips black and not showing lippiness. Nose black and sharp.

EYES. Almond shaped, very dark, full of fire and intelligence.

EARS. The leather long and wide, low set on, hanging close to the face.

MOUTH. Teeth white, strong and level.

NECK. Well proportioned and strong, to admit of the head being carried high and with dignity.

FOREQUARTERS. Shoulders strong and muscular, sloping well to the back. Legs set straight from shoulder, with plenty of bone and muscle.

BODY. Chest deep and moderately wide. Back short, strong, and slightly hollowed, the loins broad and muscular, the ribs well sprung and braced up.

HINDQUARTERS. Legs very muscular and bent, with the hocks well let down.

FEET. Rather small and of good shape, the toes well arched, pads thick and hard.

TAIL. Set on rather high, well carried, never curled or carried over back.

COAT. Very profuse and of good hard texture; if corded, hanging in tight, even cords; if non-corded, very thick and strong of even length, the curls close and thick without knots or cords. It is strongly recommended that the traditional Lion Clip should be adhered to.

COLOUR. All black, all white, all brown, all blue, and all solid colours. The white Poodle should have dark eyes, black nose, lips, and toe-nails. The brown Poodle should have dark amber eyes, dark liver nose, lips, and toe-nails. The blue Poodle should be of even colour, and have dark eyes, lips, and toe-nails. All the other points of white, brown, and blue Poodles should be the same as the perfect black Poodle.

WEIGHT AND SIZE. Fifteen inches and over.

POODLE (MINIATURE)

The Miniature Poodle should be in every respect a replica, in miniature, of the Standard Poodle. Height at shoulder should be under 15in.

FAULTS. In the Miniature Poodle: heavy build, clumsiness, long back, light, round and prominent eyes, bad stern carriage, heavy gait, coarse head, over or undershot mouth, flesh-coloured nose, coarse legs and feet, open and rusty coats, white markings of black and coloured Poodles, lemon or other markings on white Poodles.

APPENDIX II

POODLE CLUBS OF GREAT BRITAIN

THE POODLE CLUB. The first and oldest Poodle Club in England; founded originally for large Poodles in 1876. Holds a Championship Show in London annually in the autumn, and offers many special prizes for members at the principal shows. The President of the Club is H.R.H. Prince Bertil of Sweden. Hon. Secretary: Mrs. J. C. Coghlan, Fairlight, Hampton, Middlesex.

THE INTERNATIONAL POODLE CLUB. Formed in 1923 and founded by Mr. and Mrs. Campbell Inglis, offers a most interesting yearly programme for the Poodle enthusiast, including the Championship Show held in March, an Open Show later in the year, a dinner and dance annually, Christmas Party in December, a Brains Trust and many other social functions to enable members to meet visiting foreign judges. This Club also produces a most interesting bi-annual Handbook. The annual subscription is two guineas, joint subscription for partners £3 13s. 6d., and runs from July 1st to June 30th. All communications to the Secretary, Mrs. S. F. Kearns, 42 Kingscote Road, New Malden, Surrey.

THE SOUTH WESTERN POODLE CLUB. Formed in 1950 and founded by Mrs. Rothery Sheldon and Miss Lockwood. Offers many amenities to members, including a yearly Championship Show, Open Show and Members' Show; also produces a Poodle magazine, *Poodle Press*, three times a year. The annual subscription is 15/6d. for full members (22/6d. for partners) who exhibit their Poodles; and 10/6d. for members (15/6d. for partners) who do not exhibit. Members must reside within the seven counties of Cornwall, Devon, Somerset, Wiltshire, Dorset, Gloucestershire and Hampshire. Associate members outside this area 10/6d. (partners 15/6d.). All payable on January 1st. Hon. Secretary: Mr. John M. Terry, B7 Pine Grange, Bath Road, Bournemouth.

90   **POODLES**

THE TRENT TO TWEED POODLE CLUB. Formed in 1952. Offers its members a Championship Show and usually two Open Shows. Annual General Meeting and Luncheon held in October. Subscriptions: Single entrance fee 10/6d., and annual subscription 10/6d. Joint entrance fee 10/6d. and joint annual subscription 15/6d. Non-showing members annual subscription only, 10/6d. Vice-Presidents, £1 1s. The area covered is the country between the Trent and the Tweed. Hon. Secretary: Miss S. Harrold, 134 Old Road, Chesterfield. Telephone 2310.

THE MIDLAND POODLE CLUB. Formed in January, 1955. Offers its members two Open Shows per year and one Members' Show, and hopes to replace one of its Open Shows with a Championship Show when Championship status is eventually granted. Apart from catering for breeders, great stress is laid on the assistance which is offered to novices and pet owners, so that by discouraging indiscriminate breeding and encouraging careful selection and rearing, etc., there should be advantage not only to the owners but also to Poodledom in general. The subscription rates for single members are an enrolment fee of 10/6d. and an annual subscription of 10/6d. (joint members £1 1s. and 15/-). Honorary Vice-Presidents pay a minimum subscription of £1 1s. per annum. The area covered is that south of the Trent, thus "filling in" the area not covered by the T.T.P.C. to the North, S.W.P.C. to the South-West and the Poodle Club to the South-East. Hon. Secretary: Mr. Alan Booth, Claverley, near Wolverhampton.

THE NORTHERN IRELAND POODLE CLUB. Founded in 1956 by Mrs. Peacock and Miss S. Brice Smith. The aims of this Club are to encourage the showing of Poodles in Northern Ireland by procuring classes for them at shows in Northern Ireland, to run lectures, demonstrations, and social events to prove helpful to all in the care, training and full appreciation of their Poodles. Subscription 10/6d. per annum. Hon. Secretary: Miss S. Brice Smith, 54 Malone Park, Belfast, N.1. Telephone: 67071. Shows are run under English Kennel Club Rules.

THE POODLE CLUB OF IRELAND. No other details, but Hon. Secretary is Miss M. Harrison, The Shell, Delgany, Co. Wicklow, Eire. Shows are run under Irish Kennel Club Rules.

THE POODLE CLUB OF SCOTLAND. Holds Open and Members, Shows in Scotland, and is particularly diligent in securing classes for Poodles at the various Scottish Shows. The annual subscription is 10/-. Hon. Secretary: Mrs. Logan, Lyons Cross, Barrhead, near Glasgow.

THE BRITISH TOY POODLE CLUB. Founded in mid-1957. Proposes to hold regular shows for Toy Poodles. Subscription £1 1s. annually. Hon. Secretary: Miss Joan Eddie, Nashend, Bisley, Glos.

In addition to the foregoing British Clubs, there is the Poodle Club of America, which has many State Poodle Clubs affiliated to the parent body. In Europe, there is the Poodle Club of Switzerland, the Poodle Club of France, the Nederlands Poodle Club, and the Poodle Club of Sweden.

APPENDIX III

BIBLIOGRAPHY

THERE are many interesting books written for the Poodle enthusiast on all aspects of the breed, as well as many interesting monthly and weekly journals, both English and American, which contain news of Poodle activities:—

The Popular Poodle, by Alida Monro and Clara Bowring. 12/6d.
Your Poodle and Mine, by Stanley Dangerfield. 18/-.
Your Poodle, by Hayes Blake Hoyt. 10/6d.
The Book of the Poodle, by T. H. Tracy.
The Poodle, by L. F. Naylor.
The Complete Poodle, by Lydia Hopkins. (U.S.A.)

Our Dogs, published weekly. 1/-.
Dog World, published weekly. 9d.
The Kennel Club Gazette, published monthly. 3/-.
Popular Dogs (U.S.A.), published monthly. 35c.
Dog World (U.S.A.), published monthly. 35c.
The Poodle Review (U.S.A.), published monthly.

INDEX

	Page
American sizes	22
Anal Glands	28
Back	20
Balanced Diet	63
Banocide	24, 59
Barrel	20
Bathing	37
Bemax	54
Bench rugs and chains	68
Best in Show	67, 75
Bilious attacks	28
Birth of puppies	56
Blood lines	22
Breeding	44
Breeding terms	22
Brushing	36
Carrot, raw	64
Casilan	53, 57, 59
Catalogues	70
Certificate of Mating	45
Challenge Certificates	65, 66
Championship Shows	66
Changing Coat	36
Chest	20
Circuses	12, 15
Clipping	38
Clippers, Hand	43
Clippers, Electric	43
Clipper, rash	26
Coat	21, 35
Colour	16
Combs	35
Conditioning Cream	36
Continental Clip	42
Corded Poodles	12
Cowboy Trousers	40
Crufts	74, 75
Cryptorchids	21
Curly Clip	16
Dead Hair	36
Dewclaws	21, 60
Distemper	24
Dog Shows	32, 65
Dog World	67
Dosing	24
Dutch Clip	15, 39
Drying	38
Early Removals	71
Ears	16, 20, 27

	Page
Epivak	24
Exemption Shows	65
Exercise, pregnancy	55
Exercise, general	52
Eyes	20, 27
Farex	54
Feeding	61, 63
Feeding, pregnancy	53
Feet	27
First Poodle Ch.	12
Fleas	26
Free Service	50
French Clowns	15
Foundation Stock	18
Gammexane	26
Gay Tail	21
Genes	16
Gestation Period	51
Glove Puppets	79
Glucose	29, 54
Grooming	35, 36
Hard Pad	24
Heads	19
Heavy Bone	19
Hernia	57
Hindquarters	20
Hocks	20
Honey	29
House Training	29, 30
Hybrids	16
Hygiene	61
Immunization	23
Incinerators	62
Izal Powder	26
Kennel Club Registrations	12
Kennel Club Standard	16
Kennels	61
Labour pains	56
Lactol	59
Lamb Tirm	16, 39
Lead Training	31
Leathers	20
Lice	21
Limited Shows	65
Line Breeding	47
Lion Clip	15, 40

INDEX (cont.)

	Page
Loins	20
Low Set Tail	20
Lulu	79
Mating	45
Meat, Butchers	63
Meat, Knackers	64
Milton	53
Miniature Poodle	21
Misalliances	50
Mis-Marks	16
Miscarriages	55
Modern Clip	15, 39
Monorchids	21
Moustaches	39
Nails	27, 60
Obedience	82
Open Shows	65
Our Dogs	67
Outcrosses	47
Parsley	64
Parti-coloureds	16
Pedigrees	19
Pigmentation	17
Poodle Clubs	18
Poodle Management Courses	19
Premature Birth	55
Pre-whelping Preparation	52
Prices	18
Pulse	23
Punch and Judy Show	79
Puppy Clip	38
Raspberry Leaf	54
Ribs	20
Ring Numbers	71
Roach Back	30
Rothara the Rake	73, 74, 75, 78
Rothara the Riot	76
Roxie	75, 76
Runs, concrete	62
Runs, Grass	62
Runs, Gravel	62
Ry-o-tin	27
Sanction Shows	65
Schedules	67
Scissors	39, 43

	Page
Shampoos	37
Sherleys, Lactol	59
Shoulders	20
Show Equipment	67
Show Training	32, 33
Sizes	14
Slip Chains	84
Soapless Shampoos	36
Squirrel Tails	21
Standard Poodles	14, 21
Standard of the Breed	19
Sterogyl	55
Stings	27
Stud Dog, Choice of	45
Stud Dog, Proving	44
Stud Dog, Service	44
Suet	63
Suppositories	58
Tail	20
Tails, docking	60
T.C.P.	25, 53, 57
Teeth	20, 32
Teething	26
Temperament	48
Temperature	23, 56
Testicles	21
Ticks	26
Tipping of Coat	36
Toe-nails	21
Toy Poodles	12, 14, 21
Toy Poodles, American	14
Toy Box	31
Traditional Clip	15, 40
Training	29
Trimming	38
Type	47
Veterinary Examination	70
Vetzyme	24, 54
Vitacoat	37
Vitamins	61, 64
Vitamin D.	55
Washing	36
Weaning	58
Whale Hide Leads	84
Whelping	51
Whelping Quarters	51
Whelping Kennel	51